JEWS IN BARBARIAN EUROPE

by
Bernard S. Bachrach

Coronado Press   **1977**

ISBN 0–87291–088–1

Set in 10 on 12 point Press Roman
and published in the United States
of America by
Coronado Press
Box 3232
Lawrence, Kansas, 66044

FOR

Arlene, Freddy, Richard, Glen, Stephen

TABLE OF CONTENTS

INTRODUCTION

For almost two millennia, suffering has been the dominant theme in the writing of Jewish history. The dispersal of the Jews throughout Europe and the Middle East by the Roman Emperor Titus is taken as the starting point of a continuing persecution. This exile from the Holy Land is viewed as a kind of ongoing punishment that has been endured and will continue to be endured by the Jewish people until the coming of the Messiah. Within this framework, the tradition of historical writing has become firmly intertwined with what may be called the theology of Exile.

Before the development of modern historiography brought new dimensions to the study of Jewish history, those who recorded the deeds of the Jewish people during the Middle Ages and the early modern era emphasized the suffering of martyrs who died for the faith. They recorded, confounded, and embellished instances of pogroms, forced baptisms, expropriations, and expulsions. These tragic events became the framework of the Jewish view of the history of the Exile and served as evidence to sustain the theological interpretation of the Exile as a period of suffering and as a test for the Jewish people. Often, the instance of a martyrdom would be commemorated by a hymn and subsequently became integrated into the fabric of religious observance; history became liturgy and suffering an article of faith. History and theology thus reinforced each other for centuries and impressed upon both the learned and the less learned, generation upon generation, a view of the Exile that some scholars consider a lachrymose interpretation of the past.

For many learned Jews, whether professional historians or amateurs, the traditions of almost two thousand years have made it very difficult to escape the lachrymose interpretation. An effort to break with a tradition that has not only the weight of authority but also the sanction of theology is made doubly difficult by the nature of the surviving sources. As mentioned above, the Hebrew sources of a narrative character as contrasted, for example, to economic documents or responsa,* are them-

---

Responsa prudentium. In Roman Law, the responses or opinions of eminent lawyers or professional jurists on legal questions addressed to them.

selves dominated by the lachrymose bias. Thus, even the most secularly
oriented specialist in Jewish history who reads the Hebrew chronicles
which deal with the era of the First Crusade will come away with the
impression that this immense military venture launched by Pope Urban
II at the end of the eleventh century was aimed at the Jews rather than
at Islam. The reader might even come to believe that the greater part of
Western European Jewry perished in these campaigns. A careful examination of a great variety of sources in Latin and Greek as well as in Hebrew makes it clear that the accounts of the suffering endured by various Jewish communities are so overwhelmingly exaggerated in the Jewish chronicles as to give them little value as historical sources.

This lachrymose bias in the Hebrew narrative sources is given support
by the narrative sources of medieval Europe which by and large were
authored by Christian clerics who tended to view the Jews in an un-
friendly light. These sources often focus upon the deeds of those in
positions of power who took a hard line toward the Jews. In addition,
medieval clerics who wrote theology found themselves to be part of a
New Testament tradition aimed at defending Christianity against both
Jews and Judaism. Thus, Christian theological tracts provide a continuing attack of varying intensity against Jews. These texts seen together
seem to evoke an atmosphere that gives the lachrymose Jewish narrative sources the ring of truth.

The legal sources also often reinforce the same interpretation. The
canon law, for example, was, in part, intended to protect Christians
from Jews and therefore restricts both groups from productive interaction with each other. Secular law, in general, is proscriptive and thus indicates what should not be done. Thus, when one examines legislation
concerning Jews it seems that they are being singled out for unfair or
discriminatory treatment.

There are, however, a great variety of other sources such as the responsa mentioned above and documents like those found in the Cairo
Geniza which show Jewish life to be very different from what is sug-
gested by the theological tracts and law codes. Traditionally, specialists
in Jewish history and those in general medieval history who have dealt
with aspects of Jewish history have concentrated their attention on in-
tellectual and legal history. They have given comparatively little attention to social and economic history. Thus, the evidence of the law
codes and of the theological tracts has dominated the picture of the
Jewish historical experience in medieval Europe. In addition, when the
economic documents or the responsa have been studied, the tendency

has been to extract from them evidence for legal and institutional history rather than for the construction of a well-rounded picture of the whole.

The difficulties which have kept medieval Jewish history from being properly understood (both in terms of what was happening within the Jewish communities and in the relation of these communities to the Christian world in which they functioned) have been exacerbated by the apathy shown by general medievalists toward this subject. Thus, by and large, specialists in Jewish history have talked to and written for each other. This limited interaction has generally freed the ongoing debates within the field from the potentially useful criticism and contributions of those who know the medieval world from a different perspective and in a more general way. Also, specialists in Jewish history usually range over a landscape of some 5000 years of history rather than being experts, for example, in the Roman period or the early Middle Ages. This has the benefit of providing a lengthy historical perspective but also means that many who write on medieval Jewish history, even today in this age of specialization, have spread their expertise very thin. Finally, the overwhelming number of specialists in post-biblical Jewish history have been and are Jews. Among the more orthodox, the importance of the theology of the Exile is not lightly regarded. In this vein, the Holocaust may be seen to have given substantial support to those who favor the lachrymose interpretation. Even secularists can be detected to have been influenced toward an emphasis on suffering and persecution during the Middle Ages by the tragedy of the death camps.

The study of the Jews in early medieval Europe has been retarded by many of the same problems that have distorted medieval Jewish history in general. More often than not the early Middle Ages is seen as a prelude to the vigorous persecutions and violent expulsions of the later Middle Ages. Thus, in the study of the barbarian period scholars usually select from Visigothic Spain texts to illustrate the efforts of a particular monarch or church council to discriminate against Jews, convert them to Christianity, or to drive them from their homes. Within this framework each piece of anti-Jewish evidence becomes a portent of future horrors or a precedent for more widespread and vicious efforts that were to follow in a century or two centuries or even a millennium.

This approach certainly satisfies the lachrymose interpretation and clearly sustains the theology of the Exile. It fails, however, to provide an adequate understanding of the position and life of the Jews in barbarian Europe. A selection of evidence that ignores what may be considered to be the pro-Jewish aspects of a situation is simply poor history writing. More important, however, is the failure of those influenced by the lachrymose bias to grasp the significance of anti-Jewish evidence. Thus, for example, oft-repeated laws which prohibit the conversion of Christians to Judaism and an accompanying escalation of penalties strongly suggest that the laws were being broken or ignored. Such evidence may well indicate that particular lawmakers aimed at following a policy that might be construed as anti-Jewish, but the reality that underlies such a series of laws suggests that more than a few Christians were converting to Judaism despite the laws and increased penalties.

⊕

The documents presented here in translation are drawn from a great variety of sources in several languages and deal with the period from the fall of the Roman Empire to the end of the ninth century. The geographical focus is Western Europe. The world which these documents illustrate and illuminate may well be called Barbarian Europe because most of what had been the western part of the Roman Empire was during this period ruled by one or another barbarian king. In what is today France and western Germany two dynasties, the Merovingians and the Carolingians, succeeded in dominating the political scene. The Iberian peninsula was ruled during much of the early Middle Ages by the Visigoths. Their kingdom was destroyed during the early eighth century by the Muslims. In Italy the situation was more complex. First, the Ostrogoths ruled the peninsula and then the Byzantines conquered it. The Byzantine conquest was short-lived, however, and the Lombards came to dominate most of Italy by the end of the sixth century. There do not seem to have been any Jews in England during this period.

In this barbarian world three traditions came together: the Roman, the Christian and the Germanic. The Romans conquered the Jews and dispersed them throughout the empire. After the conquest, the Jews were treated much in the same manner as the other peoples who were integrated into the fabric of imperial society. In some instances the Jews were, in fact, given special treatment and received privileges that other peoples in the empire did not receive. When Christianity gained the upper hand within the empire, however, the position of the Jews like that of all other non-Christians was seriously compromised. Laws were passed aimed at limiting Jewish activities and designed to protect Christians from Jewish proselytizing. With the dissolution of the Roman Empire in the West, the church worked toward influencing the barbarian kings to pursue policies that would diminish the attractiveness of Judaism to both Jews and non-Jews. In a sense, the history of the Jews in early Medieval Europe reflects an important chapter in the struggle waged by the church to wield both the sword of spiritual power and that of secular power.

Whereas the church saw the Jews as adherents of a religion which was opposed to Christianity and as a threat to it, the Germanic rulers tended to view the Jews as a people with its own law and customs which merited the same kind of treatment and respect as did any other people. The Jews' religion was seen to be one of their more important customs and intimately connected to their law. Thus, while the church worked to limit Jewish life in a very severe manner and in some places sought to eliminate Judaism entirely, the Germanic monarchs generally did not support ecclesiastical efforts.

⊕

The materials included in this volume are divided into three broadly defined groups. The first group of texts are drawn from law codes. In studying these, students will note that most of the laws concerning Jews were intended to keep them from exercising power over Christians. Also, students will be struck by the repetitious nature of much of the legislation. This should encourage questions concerning the effectiveness of the efforts that were intended to circumscribe the activities of the Jews.

In the second group of texts a large variety of source-genres have been called upon to provide insight into the realities of Jewish life in barbarian Europe and to provide a basis for arriving at an understanding of Jewish-Christian relations during the period. These texts generally illustrate or recount events that actually took place and the context in which they are presented often makes it clear whether these occurrences were commonplace or rare. Thus, students will find it instructive to compare the accounts of actual events with the laws so as to obtain some idea of the value of the legal evidence.

The third group of texts are essentially polemical in nature and are intended to illustrate some of the basic differences that separated Jews and Christians during this era. The depth of feeling and the fundamental nature of the attacks levied by Jews against Christians and Christians against Jews should be taken as a serious representation of religious thought.

⊕

During the past decade interest in Jewish studies and particularly in Jewish history has seen an explosive development in American colleges and universities. Curiously, however, the publication of basic works needed for teaching undergraduate courses has not kept pace with the demand. The present work was undertaken because while searching for original source materials to assign to my students in an undergraduate course in Jewish-Christian relations during the early Middle Ages I was unable to find a suitable collection. This volume has been published for the express purpose of making available to undergraduate students a substantial portion of the primary sources illustrative of Jewish history in Barbarian Europe.

Most of the sources for this period are in Latin and Greek, languages which are not usually commanded by undergraduates in college survey courses. The complex style of many of the sources published here has made it desirable to translate them more with the aim of making them comprehensible to the present generation of college students than with the desire to produce a literal rendition of an obscure text into even more arcane English. These translations have a clearly interpretative intent. This is particularly the case with some legal and theological materials where it would be fair to characterize the rendition as a paraphrase rather than a translation. Some of the texts have been substantially edited. This was done in some cases in the interest of conserving space and in other cases to exclude extraneous material that might confuse the student. The usual editorial procedure of adding . . . or . . . . to mark edited sections has been avoided for cosmetic purposes.

In following the procedure described above, I have kept in mind, first and foremost, the needs of undergraduates with little or no knowledge of the period or its problems. On the whole, scholars and scholars in training (graduate students) may be expected to know the sources in the original and thus cannot be assumed to have need of the present work. They may, however, find some of the interpretations useful and for this reason reference has been made to the editions of the sources.

Θ

ROMAN BACKGROUND

Although the political power of the Roman Empire in the West declined rapidly during the later fifth century and all but disappeared during the sixth, many of its institutions survived and even flourished in barbarian Europe. One of the most enduring aspects of Roman civilization was its law. Those peoples who had been subject to the Roman law while the empire survived in the West continued to live under its aegis when the barbarian kingdoms were established. Within this system the Jews were considered to be Romans.

In 438, the Roman Emperor Theodosius II had his officials collect the laws issued by the various emperors beginning with Constantine the Great's legislation in 313. This legislation was compiled in the *Codex Theodosianus*. From 438 until 468 additions were made to the *Theodosian Code*. These were called *novellae*. More than fifty laws or sections of laws in this code and its additions deal with the Jews and stipulate treatment for them that differentiates them from other Romans. These laws concern the behavior of Jews and also the behavior to be followed by non-Jews toward Jews. The laws in the former category may be considered Roman Jewry Law, i.e. legislation especially issued by non-Jews to regulate the activities of Jews defined thereby as a group distinct from others. This Jewry law is to be contrasted with Jewish law, which is law made by Jews themselves to regulate their lives as a distinct group.

In the later Roman Empire the Jews lived under a rather complicated set of legal arrangements. Within the Jewish community, they lived under Jewish law. In relations between non-Jewish Romans and Jews who were considered to be Romans, the Jews were regulated by Roman law. In some fifty particular instances, as noted above, Jews were distinguished from other Romans by Roman Jewry law.

A substantial portion of the Roman Jewry law as well as of Roman law intended to regulate non-Jews in their relations with Jews which was collected in the *Theodosian Code* and its additions appear in

the following pages. Students will want to examine this material so as
to be able to distinguish between the two types of legislation mentioned
above. In addition, students should note that these laws contain substantial contradictions. On the whole, this selection of laws should provide
a reasonably good picture of the ways in which the governments during
the later Roman Empire distinguished between Jews and non-Jews.

SELECTIONS FROM THE THEODOSIAN CODE[1]

1. In cases that concern the Roman state as contrasted to those that
concern the Jewish superstition, Jews are to live under Roman law and
are to bring suit and defend themselves according to the Roman law. In
short, the Jews are under our laws. In cases of a civil nature, however,
Jews are permitted, if both parties agree, to have their cases decided before Jewish judges. The judges of the provinces are to carry out the decisions of these Jewish courts.

All Jews who are known to be Romans are to have the cases that
concern their religion handled by their judges and among themselves
the Jews are to live according to Jewish Law. In cases that concern the
state, Jews are to have their cases heard in the provincial court before
the imperial judge according to the laws under which everyone else
lives. (2.1.10).

2. Jewish men are not permitted to marry Christian women and Christian men are not permitted to marry Jewish women. Any person who
breaks this law is to be considered to have committed adultery. Anyone
may accuse those guilty of such acts and the judges are to pay attention
to rumors concerning these matters. (3.7.2).

3. We order that no Jew is to be compelled to do public work and no
Jew is to be brought into court on the Sabbath or on any other day
that is considered holy to that religion. Indeed, there are enough other
days in the year when Jews can perform their public services and engage
in private lawsuits. (8.8.8).

4. It is ordered that the edict cited by Jews to claim that they have immunity from performing the public services that are required from
decurions is to be cancelled. Indeed, even priests must perform the
compulsory public services that they owe to their cities before they
carry out their religious duties. (12.1.99).

5. It has come to our attention that most of the local governments in the cities of Apulia and Calabria are about to be ruined financially because the Jews claim that they are immune from performing compulsory public services. The Jews say that they hold this immunity because of a law that was issued in the Eastern part of the empire. If, in fact, this law does exist we hereby declare that it is to have no effect in our half of the empire because it is causing a great deal of difficulty here. Thus, any man who is required to perform public service to his city government according to our laws is, regardless of his religion, to perform what he owes. (12.1.158).

6. Christians who illegally have joined synagogues are hereby deprived of the right to make testaments. In addition, these people who by their shameful behavior have rejected the honor of Christianity and the name of Christian and have defiled themselves with the poison of the Jewish religion are to be punished. (16.7.3).

7. This law makes it illegal for Jews, their elders, and their patriarchs to stone or to attack any person who has left the disgusting Jewish superstition and has become a Christian. We have issued this law because at the present time such violence is carried out. Further, we order that the attackers are to be burned. Also, anyone who becomes a Jew and attends their gatherings is to receive the punishments that he deserves. (16.8.1).

8. Any man who devotes himself fully to service in the synagogues of the Jews either as a patriarch or as a priest and lives according to the laws of the Jews and presides over the administration of the Jewish law is to continue to be exempt from all compulsory public services that are owed normally to the cities. Also, if any of these persons at this time happens to be a member of a city council he is not to be assigned duty as an official escort. This is because such people are not to be forced to leave the place where they live. In addition, any of these officials who are not members of the city council are to be exempt from that duty for life. (16.8.2).

9. We permit all city governments to nominate Jews to serve in their respective city governments. In order to permit Jews to maintain some of their former exemptions we order that some Jews from each city are to continue to hold the privilege of not having to serve on the city council. (16.8.3).

10. We order that Rabbis, the heads of synagogues, the elders of synagogues, and everyone else who serves the synagogues are to be free from
all compulsory public services of a physical kind. (16.8.4).

11. Jews are not to be permitted to harass or to attack any man who
has been converted from Judaism to Christianity. Anyone who violates
this law is to be punished according to the offense of which he is guilty.
(16.8.5).

12. This edict concerns those women who once worked in the imperial
weaving factory and who have been converted to Judaism by Jewish
proselytizers. We order that they are to be returned to the weaving factory. Also, it is to be illegal for Jews to convert Christian women to
Judaism. Jews who violate this law are to be executed. (16.8.6).

13. We order in accordance with the already established ancient law
that any person who is converted from Christianity to Judaism and who
attends their religious services is to have his property confiscated and
handed over to the treasury. (16.8.7).

14. It has come to our attention that Jews are complaining that individuals who have been ousted from the Jewish community according to
Jewish law and by the Jewish authorities have been illegally restored to
their former place by imperial officials. We order this to stop. No Jew is
to be restored to his community by provincial officials or by fraudu-
lently obtained imperial orders if these contradict the orders given by
Jewish judges who hold their power from the noble and illustrious
patriarchs. (16.8.8).

15. It is well known that no law prohibits the practice of the Jewish religion. Thus, we are very disturbed that their religious gatherings have
in certain places been prohibited. Therefore, it is to be made known
that whatever severe measures that are necessary are to be taken to stop
those people who in the name of the Christian religion dare to act un-
lawfully and try to destroy and loot synagogues. (16.8.9).

16. It is prohibited for anyone who is not a Jew to dare to set the prices
at which a Jew may sell his goods. It is just that each man has the right
to set his own prices. Thus, provincial officials are not permitted to
keep on their staffs men detailed either to regulate or to investigate

prices. The governors are to punish anyone who seeks to violate this law. (16.8.10).

17. It is a basic part of that worthless superstition that the synagogue leaders, the Jews' priests, and those whom they themselves call apostles are ordered by the patriarch at a designated time each year to collect gold and silver. This wealth is to be brought back to the patriarch and the exact amount levied is the same as that which is collected from each synagogue. Since it is clear that the whole tax will have been collected for the stipulated period, we order that it all be handed over to our treasury. Indeed, hereafter, we order that no funds are to be sent to the above-mentioned patriarch. The Jews are to be told that by this order from now on we have put an end to the collection of this tax by the patriarch. If anyone is sent out to collect this illegal tax in the future and goes on such a mission at the order of the greedy patriarch who squeezes the Jews of the empire, the tax collectors are to be tried by imperial judges under imperial law and are to be sentenced for breaking our laws. (16.8.14).

18. We order that the privileges that previous emperors have granted to the patriarchs of the Jews and to the men to whom the patriarchs have delegated their authority are to remain in force. (16.8.15).

19. We order that the Jews and the Samaritans who are members of the secret service are to give up this privilege and that they are not to be employed in any way in the imperial government. (16.8.16).

20. We decreed earlier that the taxes collected by the Jews of the empire and formerly sent to the patriarch in Jerusalem were to be handed over to us. Now we recognize that earlier emperors had granted this privilege and thus we rescind our previous order. Everyone is to know that we hereby grant to the Jews the right to collect money and to send those funds to the patriarchs in Jerusalem. (16.8.17).

21. The provincial governors are to see to it that the Jews are stopped from celebrating a ceremony during the feast of Haman in which they set on fire and burn symbols that look like the holy cross. They do this sacrilegiously to show their hatred of Christianity. They must be stopped therefore from confusing the symbol of our holy Christian faith with their own doings. They are permitted, however, to keep their

own religious ceremonies as long as they do not show hatred for Christianity. If they persist in their contemptuous behavior they will lose all of the privileges which have been granted to them. (16.8.18).

22. Certain people who have little regard for their own lives and ignore imperial law dare to force Christians to become Jews. The people who have committed these crimes have broken the laws enacted by previous emperors. We find it worthwhile, however, to warn the Jews not to dare to force Christians to convert to Judaism which is a religion that is both perverse and foreign to the Roman Empire. Anyone who thinks that he can be a proselytizer should know that he is subject along with his accomplices to the severe punishments that have already been enacted. Indeed, it is more lamentable than death and crueler than murder for any Christian to be defiled by the Jewish superstition. Anyone who breaks these laws which prohibit the converting of Christians to Judaism is guilty of high treason. (16.8.19).

23. Any place that is considered to be a Jewish meeting house which they call a synagogue is to be safe from any efforts to attack it or to occupy it or to seize possession of it. Everyone has the right to possess his own property in an undisturbed manner and no claim can be made against this right on the basis of a religious argument. In addition, according to ancient custom and habit the Jews hold the Sabbath to be holy and therefore we order that no Jew can be forced by any official order to do any public business or any private business that requires him to act contrary to his religion. Indeed, there seems to be plenty of time during the rest of the week to do what needs to be done and that the privileges of the Jews are not to be violated as indicated in the laws enacted by previous emperors. (16.8.20).

24. No person simply because he is a Jew is to suffer when he is innocent. No one is to be attacked for religious reasons. Synagogues and Jewish houses are not to be burned and Jews are not to be attacked illegally. If a Jew is shown to have been involved in criminal activity it is the job of the imperial courts to deal with the matter. Within the empire no person has the power to take revenge for himself. It should be noted, however, that just as we have set forth the above-mentioned law to protect the Jews, the latter are warned that they are not to become brazen and insolent because of the security that we have given them. Jews are not to commit any violent acts against the Christian religion. (16.8.21).

25. Gamaliel, because he was given a very high office, thought that he could act contrary to the law without being punished for doing so. Therefore, you, our governor, should know that we have sent instructions to the master of the officers depriving Gamaliel of his right to act as honorary prefect and that he is to hold only his previous office from now on. Hereafter, he is not to dare to establish any new synagogues. In addition, if there are any synagogues which are now standing in uninhabited places he should have them torn down if this can be done without causing a revolt. Further, Gamaliel no longer is to have the power to judge cases between Christians. If a case should come up between Christians and Jews it is to be decided by the governor of the province. If Gamaliel tries to convert a Christian or anyone else, free or slave, to Judaism, he is to be punished according to the law. Finally, if Gamaliel continues to hold any Christian slaves he is to give them up and they are to be handed over to the church. (16.8.22).

26. It is contrary to both ancient laws and our own laws for Jews to convert to Christianity for the purpose of avoiding prosecution or for other non-religious reasons. We know that such conversions are not the result of sincere religious faith but tricks. Thus, our officials are to be very careful to see to it that our laws are enforced and to see to it that Jews who have become Christians for the above-mentioned reasons should be treated as Jews under their own law. (16.8.23).

27. From now on all those who live according to the Jewish religion are to be kept from entering imperial service. Those who have already sworn the oaths for service in the secret service or for the staff of the imperial palace we permit to finish out their period of enlistment. This is not intended to favor Jews in such positions but to ignore the problem for the present. In the future, however, this law is to be enforced without exception. It should be noted, however, that we do not prohibit Jews who have been trained in the liberal arts from serving as lawyers. In addition, we do allow them the honor of performing compulsory public services as members of city governments since they have obtained this right as a result of their birth and the position of their family. The privileges noted above should be enough for the Jews and they are not to consider that they are being harmed or degraded because we no longer permit them to serve in the imperial service. (16.8.24).

28. We order that no Jewish synagogue is to be burned or confiscated without due cause. If there are any synagogues which recently have

been given to churches or to other religious groups the Jews are to receive compensation. In addition, the Jews are permitted to build new
synagogues similar to the old ones which were taken from them. If any
religious symbols, books, or other things have been taken they are to be
returned unless thay have been made a part of their new owner's cult.
In the latter case the Jews are to receive compensation so that they can
replace the lost goods. From now on, however, no new synagogues are
to be built and already existing ones are to remain in the condition in
which they are in at present. (16.8.25).

29. The recent laws concerning Jews and their synagogues are to remain
in force. Jews are not to build new synagogues but their possession of
already existing synagogues is to be protected. (16.8.27).

30. No Jewish father or mother or grandfather or grandmother is permitted to omit from their testaments or to disinherit any son or daughter or grandson or granddaughter because they have given up the be-
nighted Jewish religion and because of wise counsel have converted to
Christianity. In addition, such converts are not to be left less in a testament than they would have received if the estate were declared intestate. If a Jew violates this law then the testament is to be declared null
and void. The estate is to be treated as though the person had died
intestate. (16.8.28).

31. If a Jew buys a slave who is not a Jew then that slave is to be handed over to the imperial treasury immediately. If a Jew buys a Christian
slave and circumcises him, the slave is to be confiscated and the owner
is to be executed. A Jew who buys Christian slaves must give up all of
the Christian slaves that are in his possession at once. There must be no
delay in confiscating from the possession of Jews any Christian slaves
whom they hold illegally. (16.9.2).

32. We order that it is legal for Jewish owners to possess Christian slaves
without fearing that some kind of trickery is involved. The single condition is that the slave be permitted to keep his own religion. Thus,
throughout the empire the proper officials are to examine all complaints against Jewish slave owners who own Christian slaves. Further,
let it be known that these officials are to stop those who bring unjust
accusations against Jews for personal gain. (16.9.3).

33. Jews are not permitted to buy Christian slaves or to obtain them as gifts. Any Jew who breaks this law is to have the slave in question confiscated. If the slave provides the information that leads to the discovery that the law has been broken then he is to be given his freedom. A Jew, however, is permitted to continue to keep all other Christian slaves whom he already owned even though they are of the true faith and he is the follower of a hated superstition. This condition refers only to slaves that the Jew had obtained before the law went into effect and includes those Christian slaves that he might inherit or obtain through a trust. Further, the Jew will lose the slaves if either by force or by other means he converts these slaves to Judaism. If Jewish slave owners do convert their Christian slaves to Judaism, the lawbreakers are to be executed and their property is to be confiscated. (16.9.4).

34. We order that people who are Christians or who say that they are Christians are not to use their religion as an excuse to attack law-abiding Jews or pagans who do not disturb the peace. Any Christian who attacks the above-mentioned people who live under imperial protection is to return the property that was stolen and is to pay damages three or four times the value of what he took. Indeed, if any imperial official connives in this illegal activity he too is subject to the same punishment as those who have committed the crimes. (16.10.24).

35 We prohibit Jews and pagans from pleading cases and from holding government positions. Christian slaves are not to be owned by Jews. Jews are not to use their rights as slave owners to convert their slaves to Judaism. (Sirm. 6).

36. If any Jew holds an imperial office he is to give it up. If a Jew builds a synagogue it is to be confiscated and handed over to the Catholic church. Any Jew who starts to build a new synagogue is to be fined fifty pounds of gold and is to have the land and building confiscated. In addition, if he tries to convert Christians to Judaism his property is to be confiscated and he is to be executed. (Nov. Th. 3.1.5).

37. Neither Jews nor Samaritans are to be permitted to obtain any position or office in the imperial government. They are not permitted to hold the office of defender of the city or to serve as prison guards. We order this to keep Jews from using such offices to harass Christians and clerics and to keep Jews from holding positions in which they as ene-

mies of our law might dare to punish or judge someone who is subject to our law. Further, no Jew is to dare to convert a Christian, free or slave, to Judaism by any means. If a Jew does this he is to have his property confiscated and he is to be executed. (Nov. Th. 3.1.9).

CANON LAW

In a strict technical sense it is probably not accurate to characterize the canons enacted by church councils during the early Middle Ages as Canon Law. Nevertheless, in many circumstances these canons had the force of law for the regulation of the behavior of Christians, and in addition the ecclesiastical lawyers who codified canon law later in the Middle Ages frequently incorporated these enactments or versions of them into their collections.

Substantial numbers of canons that were enacted during the early Middle Ages concern Jews. The frequency with which the councils acted with regard to Jews depended upon a great variety of circumstances and each situation presents the student with a unique historical problem. Sometimes the ecclesiastical magnates were asked by the secular powers to enact canons concerning Jews and at other times the councils took the initiative in the hope of influencing the secular government. Like the Roman law discussed above, the canons concerning Jews can to a certain extent be categorized according to whose behavior they were intended to regulate. There are laws aimed at regulating the behavior of Christians toward Jews. These canons could be enforced by the church through spiritual sanctions such as excommunication. There were also canons that were intended to regulate the activities of the Jews. This type of legislation can be called canon Jewry law. The canon Jewry law could be enforced only by those who wielded secular power. It should be noted that on occasion ecclesiastics of high rank such as bishops and abbots also held important positions of secular responsibility. Thus, if they were so inclined such ecclesiastics were in a position to enforce canon Jewry law.

The canons that are presented here represent only a small portion of the many that were promulgated concerning Jews by early Medieval church councils. They include selections from Visigothic Spain[2] and Frankish Gaul.[3] In studying these texts students will want to examine the legislation closely so as to be able to identify the Jewry provisions and also to see what a wide variety of subjects came within the scope of conciliar legislation. Particular attention should be paid to the repetition of particular enactments and what may seem to be contradictions embodied within the canons.

FOURTH COUNCIL OF TOLEDO–633

1. This holy council orders that Jews are not to be forced to accept our beliefs. Rather, the Jews are to be persuaded to accept Christianity by their free will and not by force. Those, however, who were forced to accept Christianity in the days of the very pious ruler Sisebut are to remain Christians. (c.57).

2. Any bishop, cleric, or layman who protects Jews either in return for gifts or in return for the use of their influence so that the Christian faith is harmed is to be anathematized. (c.58).

3. Any Jew who has accepted the Christian faith but who continues to practice Jewish rites is to be corrected by the priests. Those who circumcise their own children are to have these children taken from them and those who circumcise their slaves are to lose them and the slaves are to be freed. (c.59).

4. In order to keep the sons and daughters of Jews from being contaminated by their parents' errors we order that these children are to be taken from their parents. These children are to be sent to monasteries or to God-fearing Christian men and women so that they will learn to honor the true faith and become proficient in the customs of Christianity. (c.60).

5. If a Jew who has been baptized returns to the practice of Judaism and is subsequently punished, his children who remained good Christians are not to lose their inheritance. (c.61).

6. There is to be no contact between Jews who have become Christians and those Jews who continue to practice their faith. This is to keep the former from being polluted by the latter. If, however, the former do not obey this law they are to be handed over to Christians who will beat them in public. (c.62).

7. Jews who have Christian wives are to be told by the bishop of the diocese in which they live that they must convert to Christianity. If they refuse to do this then they are to be separated because a woman who has become a Christian cannot live with a man who is a Jew. Children who have been born into such marriages are to be raised in the mother's faith. Children who are born into a family where the mother is a Jew and the father is a Christian are to follow the Christian religion and not the Jewish superstition. (c.63).

8. Jews who were at one time Christians but now have rejected the faith of Christ are not to be permitted to act as witnesses even if they now say that they are Christians. (c.64).

9. Jews are not to hold public offices because they would be in a position to treat Christians unjustly. Thus, judges in the various districts are to work with the priests to see to it that no Jew obtains such an office illegally or holds it by fraud. Any judge who permits Jews to do this is to be excommunicated and the Jew is to be beaten in public. (c.65).

10. It is illegal for Jews to own Christian slaves, or to buy Christian slaves, or to obtain Christian slaves as a gift. Any Christian slave, male or female, in the possession of a Jew, is to be freed immediately. (c.66).

SIXTH COUNCIL OF TOLEDO–638

1. No one is to become king before he has sworn that he will not permit the Jews to attack the Catholic faith and that he will not do anything that in any way might favor the Jews either because of neglect or because of greed. If he fails to live up to his oath after he has taken over the government then he is to be anathematized. (c.3).

TENTH COUNCIL OF TOLEDO–656

1. The canons prohibit any Jew from daring to have any Christian salves or Christian wives. (c.7).

TWELFTH COUNCIL OF TOLEDO–681

1. The council promulgates as canons the king's laws concerning Jews and reaffirms the previous laws enacted against the Jews.

a. Affirmed, the law against those who blaspheme against the Holy Trinity.

b. Affirmed, Jews are not to avoid baptism themselves nor are they to keep their children or their slaves from being baptized.

c. Affirmed, the Jews are not to celebrate Easter according to their rituals, they are not to practice circumcision, they are not to convert anyone from Christianity to Judaism.

d. Affirmed, the Jews are not to dare to celebrate the Sabbath or any of their religious holidays.

e. Affirmed, the Jews are not to work on Sunday or on any Christian holiday.

f. Affirmed, no Jew is to follow Jewish dietary customs.

g. Affirmed, no Jew is permitted to marry a close relative nor dare to marry without the blessing of a priest.

h. Affirmed, no Jew is to dare to defend his sect and insult ours. No Jew is to flee to avoid being a Christian and no one is to dare to aid such a person who does flee.

i. Affirmed, no Christian is to accept a gift from a Jew if in any way this can be seen to harm the Christian faith.

j. Affirmed, no Jew is to dare to read any books that repudiate the Christian faith.

k. Affirmed, Christian slaves are not to work for or belong to Jews.

l. Affirmed, if a Jew claims to be a Christian so that he can avoid giving up his slaves he is not to be permitted to get away with this.

m. Affirmed, every Jew who becomes a Christian is to make a profession of faith in writing.

n. Affirmed, the clauses sworn to by Jews who become Christians are to conform to those made by those professing the true faith.

o. Affirmed, the laws concerning Christian slaves who belong to Jews and who have not become Christians and also the laws regarding those who denounce the latter.

p. Affirmed, no Jew is to dare to command, punish, or imprison any Christian except at the command of the king.

q. Affirmed, those slaves who have not yet become Christians and who are owned by Jews are to be freed if they become Christians.

r. Affirmed, Jews are not to serve as administrators in charge of groups of Christian slaves. Jews are not to be given authority either by slave owners or by governmental officials to administer the work of slaves on either private lands or on public lands. Those who break these laws are to be punished.

s.   Affirmed, any Jew who comes from any province or territory
      that is part of this kingdom is to go immediately to the local
      bishop in order to be told what is required of him.

t.   Affirmed, the legal manner in which the bishop is to gather to-
      gether the Jews on appropriate days.

u.   Affirmed, anyone who has a Jewish dependent is to present him
      to the bishop or priest upon request and dare not disobey.

v.   Affirmed, all punishment of Jews is to be left to the priests.

w.   Affirmed, all the penalties that are to be imposed upon priests
      and judges who fail to enforce the laws concerning the Jews.

x.   Affirmed, the Judges are not to dare to handle any cases relative
      to the abuses committed by unfaithful Jews without a priest tak-
      ing part in the action.

y.   Affirmed, the bishops are not to be liable for punishment if the
      priests under them have not informed them about abuses that
      they have not corrected.

z.   Affirmed, every bishop is to provide to the Jews living in his dio-
      cese a little book concerning the errors of the Jewish superstition.
      The bishops are also to keep in their archives the professions of
      faith and the sworn promises that were made by the Jews. (The
      above 26 stipulations are found in canon 9).

SEVENTEENTH COUNCIL OF TOLEDO–694

1. The Jews who tried to overthrow King Egica are to be deprived of all
of their goods and all of their possessions are to be confiscated. This is
to be the punishment of these traitors, of their wives, and also of their
descendants. They are to be taken from their homes and dispersed
throughout the provinces of Spain. They are to be punished with perpetual slavery as the possessions of persons chosen by the king. Under
no pretext are they to recover their freedom since they remain obsti-
nate in their infidelity and because they are infamous for their many
crimes. (c.8).

SECOND COUNCIL OF ORLEANS–533

1. It is established that no Christian man is to marry a Jewish woman
and that no Jewish man is to marry a Christian woman. We decree that
a marriage among these people is illegal. (c.19).

COUNCIL OF CLERMONT–535

1. No Jews are to be placed as judges or as other lower officials over Christians. (c.9).

THIRD COUNCIL OF ORLEANS–539

1. If Christian slaves who are owned by Jews are ordered by their owners to do something that is prohibited by the Christian religion and if the owner dares to beat or perhaps even tries to kill them for this disobedience which the church permits and if the slaves then flee to the church, no priest is to hand them back over to their owners unless the price of the slave is offered and this is given according to the appraisal that will have been made. Also, we order that all Christians are forbidden to marry Jews. If they do this they are to be cast out of Christian society and driven away from communion. Also, we forbid Christians to eat with Jews. If someone is shown to have done this he is to be excommunicated for a year. (c.14).

2. Because Christians have been shown to observe the Jewish superstitions with regard to the Sabbath so that they do not ride horses, harness oxen to carts nor prepare meals nor clean their houses, nor do any kind of work we order that all of this work is permitted to Christians who are not to follow Jewish customs. (c.28).

3. From Holy Thursday up until the second day after Easter Saturday, that is four days in all, Jews are not to be in the company of Christians and the Catholic people are not to mix in any way with Jews. (c.33).

FOURTH COUNCIL OF ORLEANS–541

1. We order that any Jew who converts a pagan to the Jewish superstition, or who converts someone who previously had been a Christian to Judaism, or who takes as his wife a female Christian slave, or who converts to Judaism someone who was born of Christian parents is to lose all of his slaves. If a slave born of Christian parents becomes a Jew so that he may become free this arrangement is to have no force. Indeed, anyone who was born of Christian parents and who wishes to become a Jew should not be free. (c.31).

FIFTH COUNCIL OF ORLEANS–548

1. If a slave is guilty of wrongdoing and flees to a church the priest is not to give him back unless the owner promises by an oath to pardon him. If the owner does not pardon the slave then he is to be excommunicated. If after the master has taken the oath the slave refuses to leave the church then the owner is permitted to take him by force. If the owner is a pagan or a Jew then he is to have with him worthy Christians to support his oath to pardon the slave. (c.22).

COUNCIL OF MÂCON–583

1. Jews are not to enter the convents of nuns for any reason or any kind of business or to have any conversations with nuns or to be familiar with them whether secretly or otherwise. (c.2).

2. Jews are not to be appointed as judges over Christians and they are not to be permitted to be tax collectors. God forbid that Christians may become subject to Jews! (c.13).

3. No Christian is to dare to take part in the feasts held by Jews. Those who do so are to be excommunicated. (c.15).

4. If a Jew is found to have persuaded a Christian slave to accept the errors of Judaism then he is to lose the slave and he is to be punished according to the law. (c.17).

COUNCIL OF PARIS–614

1. No Jew is to dare to serve in any governmental office or to carry out any public duty in which he exercises power over Christians. Jews are not to seek such positions from the king. If a Jew is seen to have carried out such duties he is to be baptized along with his entire family by the bishop of the diocese in which this violation of the canon took place. (c. 17)

COUNCIL OF RHEIMS–627

1. Christians are not to be sold to Jews or to pagans. If a Christian believes that it is necessary to sell a slave then that slave is to be sold only to another Christian. If the slave is sold to a Jew or to a pagan then the seller is to be excommunicated and the sale is to be voided. Indeed, if Jews dare to convert Christian slaves to Judaism or if they punish them very cruelly then the slave is to be turned over to the royal treasury. Also Jews are not to carry out any governmental business. Christians are forbidden to attend the feasts of the Jews. (c.11).

GERMANIC LAW

As we have seen, the Jews were considered to be Romans according to the Roman law in their relations with Romans who were not Jews. When the Germanic kingdoms were established in what had been the western part of the Roman Empire, however, a substantial number of Germanic peoples, each with its own law, brought a new dimension to the legal situation. Means had to be established not only for the interaction under law of the various Germanic peoples but regulations had to be developed concerning the relation of the Germanic peoples to the Romans.

With regard to the Jews, the various Germanic kingdoms were faced with a complex situation. When the Jews were looked at in their own communities they appeared to be much like any other people who lived according to its own law, i.e. Jewish law. The only major difference between the Jews and the various Germanic peoples is that the former were not Christian even in a nominal way as were the latter. When, however, the Jews were considered in relation to the various non-Germanic peoples they were clearly Romans because according to the Roman law, as noted above, the Jews lived under Roman law in their relation with non-Jewish Romans. In addition to the substantial body of Roman Jewry law that complicated the position of the Jews as Romans still further, there was also a growing body of canon Jewry law.

The church often tried to influence the Germanic rulers to develop Jewry law that was consistent with the canons. Since throughout most of the early Middle Ages these kings were orthodox Christians, the task of the church was somewhat simplified. Yet, the canon Jewry law was often at odds with the Roman Jewry law. Further, the interests of the various monarchs were such that from time to time neither the Jewry provisions of the canon law nor those of the Roman law suited their aims. Thus, in the development of Germanic Jewry law there can be detected, depending upon circumstances, the influence of canon law and Roman law as well as the policies of the monarchs themselves. On occasion one can even detect the influence of Jewish law in the development of Germanic Jewry law.

The texts presented here have been selected from the laws promulgated by various Germanic rulers in the Visigothic kingdom, the Burgundian kingdom, and the Frankish kingdoms. In studying this legislation the reader will want to seek out the influence which inspired a particular enactment and should try to understand the circumstances that brought them into being. It is important also to look for contradictions, repetitions, and escalation of penalties.

SELECTIONS FROM THE LAWS OF THE VISIGOTHS[4]

KING RECCARED I (586-681)

1. A Jew is not permitted to buy a Christian slave or to receive one as a gift. If a Jew does buy a Christian slave or if he receives one as a gift and then circumcises him, the Jew is to lose the price he paid for the slave and the latter is to be freed. Also, any Jew who circumcises a Christian slave is to have his property confiscated by the royal treasury. Moreover, any male or female slave who does not want to become a Jew is to be freed. (XII.2.12).

KING SISEBUT (612-621)

To the holy and blessed bishops Agapius, Cecilius, and the other Agapius and to the counts in their districts and similarly to the remaining priests and counts in the territories of Castillon, Jaen, los Villares, las Cuevas de Lituergo, Baeza, Toya, la Balera, Cabra, and Aguilar de la Frontera.

1. The law established by King Reccared, our predecessor, making it illegal for a Christian slave to remain under the control of Hebrews would have been sufficient if the Jews had not in their perversity swayed the magnates and acquired illegal concessions. Therefore, with God's help we nullify Reccared's law so that the Jews' cheating will be stopped and we establish that any Christian slave who is not in the possession of Jews whether he should have been freed under Reccared's law or not is now to be freed and to have the rights enjoyed by a Roman citizen.

2. If a Christian slave is sold by his Jewish owner under a written contract illegally after this law is established, the slave is to be freed and the contract is to be voided. The sellers are to return the money they obtained. The freed slave is to have his name recorded as a free man and he is to live freely according to his own labor and pay his just share of the taxes.

3. If any Jews acquire Christian slaves in a legal manner between the establishment of this law and the first of July they have the right to sell them or to set them free.

4. Any Christian slaves who have been circumcised by the Hebrews and at any time have taken part in their rituals are to be punished according to the law.

5. Any Hebrew who first frees a Christian slave and then enslaves him again or who keeps a Christian slave and does not free him according to our law is not to delay in making reparation to the slave according to the laws governing the enslavement of free men.

6. All Jews who have converted to Christianity are to receive the share of their parents' Christian slaves that would normally go to an heir.

7. Any Jew who is shown to have obtained anything in an illegal manner from our predecessors is to lose it to the royal treasury.

8. Any Jewish-owned slaves who have been baptized and have fled from their owners are to be returned to the latter so that they can free them according to the law and give them their property. Those slaves who do not have any property are to be given some by their former owner. Then these freed slaves are to be listed on the tax lists along with other freed slaves and pay taxes to the treasury on their property. (XII.2.13).

SISEBUT

We bring healthful remedies to all the peoples who live in the provinces of our kingdom and to the Goths when we take Christians out of the hands of the unfaithful. In this way the orthodox rule of faith will be glorified and the cursed treachery of the Hebrews will not have any power over Christians. The stinking power of the Jews over Christians is to be hated and the people consecrated by God's grace are to be led back to Catholic love.

1. Therefore, we establish in perpetuity and make clear to all palace officials for the future that beginning in the first year of our reign no Hebrew is to have a free Christian under his patronage or a Christian slave in his service nor are Jews permitted to hire any Christians or utilize the services of Christians for any reason at all.

2. A Jew is permitted, however, to sell his Christian slaves within the boundaries of our kingdom where he dwells along with the slave's property at a just price.

3. It is not permitted to sell slaves outside the regions in which they live unless it can be proved that the slaves were from that area originally.

4. When a slave is sold to someone outside of the local region then he is to be provided by the seller with enough property to feed and clothe him so that it is clear that a sale was being carried out and that the slave was not being exiled.

5. When a Hebrew frees a Christian slave he must do so in a way that enables him to assume the position of a Roman citizen. Thus no services are to be owed to the Hebrew or to anyone else by the erstwhile slave. The freed slave thus has the right to live where he wants and no longer owes anything to the Jew who freed him.

6. If a Hebrew engages in a fraud with regard to the sale of a Christian slave and this is discovered, the person who provides the information, if he is a free man, is to receive all of the property of both the buyer and the seller who engaged in the fraud. If one of the parties to the fraud is a free Christian he is to be enslaved and handed over to someone designated by the king. The man who perpetrates such a fraud is to lose half of his goods to the royal treasury. If a slave provides the information that leads to proving the fraud, he is to be set free under the patronage of his owner. So that the owner does not lose anything he will be given a slave from the royal treasury and a pound of gold from the estate of those who perpetrated the fraud.

7. If a Hebrew circumcises a Christian man or converts a Christian woman to the Jewish sect and its ceremonies the Jew is to be executed

and his property is to be handed over to the royal treasury. All slaves who are known to have been born from the union of a Christian and a Jew are to be considered Christians. If these slaves have already been converted to the religion of the Hebrews and they wish to remain in that treacherous state they are to be beaten, have their heads shaved in public, and they are to be handed over to be slaves forever to someone chosen by the king.

9. Concerning the illegal marriages of Jews and Christians, discussed above, it is permitted for the Jewish partner to become a Christian and thus to preserve the marriage. If the Jewish partner refuses to become a Christian then as a penalty the guilty party is to suffer perpetual exile.

10. In addition, we order that all Hebrews who make a profession of faith, become good Catholics, and undergo the purification of baptism are to remain in possession of the property that they held before their conversion.

11. We order that this decree is to go into force for all of our subjects in all of the lands that are under our control from the first day of July of this year.

12. If after this above date any Jew is discovered to possess a Christian slave, the latter is to be set free and the Hebrew is to hand over half of his property to the royal treasury. The Hebrew also is to have no rights at all concerning either the person or the property of the slave.

13. This law which we have established for the help of our people because of our piety and love of religion is to remain in force in perpetuity with God's help.

14. Although we believe that no one will dare to break this law, anyone who does break it or who does not enthusiastically enforce it is to suffer infamy in this world and he is to suffer eternal damnation from the moment he thought to break this law. (XII.2.14).

KING CHINDASUINTH (642-653)

Because a cruel and outrageous act should be punished by an even more cruel penalty we order that if it is shown that either a Christian man or a Christian woman and especially one who is the son or daughter of Christian parents circumcises someone or practices any other Jewish ritual or anything else of this kind which God forbids he or she is to suffer a horrible death by a variety of painful tortures so that the offender will understand how truly horrible Judaizing is. All of the property that was held by such a person is to go to the royal treasury so that the heirs and relatives will also suffer because they may be seen to have been tainted by the act for not having stopped it. (XII.2.16).

KING RECCESUINTH (649-672)

1. No jew is to celebrate Passover on the fourteenth day of the month nor celebrate any customs that a Jew usually celebrates. In addition, no Jew is to celebrate any of his old holidays or to partake in the old errors whether these be small ones or big ones. Jews are not to rest on these former holidays nor are they to rest on the Sabbath. Anyone who breaks these laws or even tries to do so is to be punished according to the law.

2. No Jew is to marry or to pollute with incest or adultery anyone who is a close blood relation. Jews are not to marry anyone who is related to them to the seventh degree. They are to be married according to the Christian ceremony and they are not to use any other kind of ceremony. If they are caught breaking this law they are to be punished according to the law.

3. Jews are not permitted to perform circumcisions. A person who is circumcised also comes under this law and no slave, or free man, or highly born free person is to permit himself to undergo this hateful operation whether he is a native or a foreigner. Anyone who either performs or submits to this ritual freely is to be very harshly punished.

4. We order that no Jew is to be permitted to bear witness against any Christian in any legal proceeding of any kind. This is to be the case even if the Christian is a lowborn freeman or even a slave. Also, Jews are not permitted to bring suits against Christians or subject them to torture for any reason at all. If Jews have a reason to sue each other they are to do so and to testify against each other and torture their slaves. All this, however, is to be done before a Christian judge. (XII.2.5).

KING ERWIG (680-687)

Anyone guilty of the following offenses is to receive 100 lashes, have his hair shaved off, have his property taken by the royal treasury, and he is to be made a slave.

1. A Jew who dares to insult the Christian religion.

2. A Jew who by his arguments persuades someone to become a Jew.

3. A Jew who defends Judaism.

4. A Jew who flees to avoid baptism.

5. Anyone who offers a hiding place to a Jew who flees from Christianity. (XII.3.9).

ERWIG

Any Jew who reads books or studies doctrines that attack or deny the truth of the Christian religion and any Jew who keeps such books or hides them in his house is to receive 100 lashes and have his hair shaved off. Anyone who is guilty of breaking this law a second time is to receive 100 lashes, have his hair shaved off, and have his property taken by the king who will give it away to someone of his choice. The offender then will be exiled perpetually. Anyone who teaches the denial of Christianity to children is to receive 100 lashes, have his hair shaved off, and sign a written statement that he swears that he will never do it again. If this teacher breaks his sworn word he is to have his hair shaved off, receive 100 lashes, and have his property taken by the royal treasury. Then he is to be exiled perpetually. Children who are less than ten years of age and who have been shown to have studied these teachings are not to be punished. Any child who is more than ten years of age, however, and is guilty of the above is to be treated like an adult. (XII.3.11).

BURGUNDIAN LAW–524-532[5]

CONCERNING JEWS WHO ATTACK CHRISTIANS

1. Any Jew who dares to attack a Christian with his fists, or a shoe, a whip, or a stone, or who has pulled the hair of a Christian, is to have his hand cut off.

2. If the Jew wants to avoid losing his hand then by our order he can pay a composition of seventy-five gold pieces and a fine of twenty-five gold pieces.

3. In addition, any Jew who has dared to attack a priest is to be executed and his property is to be turned over to the royal treasury. (no. 102).

CAPITULARIES OF CHARLEMAGNE (768-814)

AND

LOUIS THE PIOUS (814-840)[6]

809

1. It is established concerning the Jews that if any one of them because of a disagreement brings a suit against a Christian and the Jew is to prove his case with witnesses, three worthy Christian witnesses suffice and he is also to have four or nine or seven Jewish witnesses according to the value of the thing in dispute. If a Christian wishes to bring suit against a Jew it is enough for him to have three worthy Christian witnesses and three Jews.

2. It is established that Jews are not to dare to hire Christian men to do their work on Sunday. If they do hire someone to work on Sunday and it is found out, the Jew is to lose the wages he has paid and the Christian is to be punished so that others will not dare to do servile work on Sunday. (no.63, ch.13).

ca. 813-814

1. Let no Jew dare to receive from the church of God anything either in gold or in silver or of any other kind either in pledge or for any debt from any Christian. Any Jew who dares to do this is to have all of his goods confiscated and his right arm cut off.

2. Let no Jew dare to take any Christian in pledge from any Jew or from another Christian lest the man pledged be lowered in status. If a Jew dares to do this he is to repay the man so lowered in status according to the latter's law. The Jew also is to lose both the debt and the pledge.

3. No Jew is to dare to have a mint in his own home or dare to sell wine or grain or other goods there. If he is discovered doing this all of his goods are to be confiscated and he is to be locked up until he can be brought into our presence.

4. Concerning the oath taken by Jews in cases involving Christians. The Jew is to wrap himself around twice from head to foot in his prayer shawl and to stand while he swears the oath. Also, he must have in his right hand the five books of Moses as indicated by his own law and if he cannot find a Hebrew version he is to use one in Latin. (no.131, chs.1-4).

TWO JEWISH OATHS

ca. 813-814

1. So God may help me, the God who gave the law to Moses on Mount Sinai, and so that the leprosy of the Syrian Naamen may not come upon me as it came on him, and so that the earth may not swallow me up as it swallowed up Dathan and Abiron, in this case I have done no evil against you. (no.131. ch.4).

ca.814-840

2. I swear to you by the living and true God and by the holy law that the Lord has given to the blessed Moses on Mount Sinai and by the

good Lord, and by the pact of Abraham that God gave to the children of Israel, and so that the leprosy of Naamen the Syrian may not cover my body, and so that the land may not swallow me up alive as it did Dathan and Abiron, and through the arc of the alliance that appears in the heavens to the children of man, and the holy place where holy Moses stood and where the blessed Moses received the holy law, I am not guilty in this case. (no.131, ch.5)

RECONSTRUCTIONS OF LOST CAPITULARIES[7]

814-840

1. Let no one presume to keep a Jewish community from building a new synagogoe.

2. Let no one presume to deprive a Jew of the right to purchase, possess, employ, or sell pagan slaves.

3. Let no one presume to punish a Jew for converting a pagan slave to Judaism.

4. Let no one presume to punish a Jew for circumcising a pagan slave.

5. Let no one presume to baptize a Jewish-owned slave without the owner's permission.

6. Let no one presume to stop Jews from employing Christian laborers.

7. Let no one permit a market to be held on the Jewish Sabbath.

ROMAN LAW IN THE GERMANIC KINGDOMS

The Theodosian Code was superseded as the law of the Roman Empire by the great compilation carried out at the command of the Emperor Justinian (527-565). The *Codex Justinianus* became the law of the land in the Eastern part of the Roman Empire and in those areas in the West that were under Byzantine domination. In the barbarian kingdoms of the West, however, the Theodosian Code continued to be used. This collection was too detailed and too complicated for the much diminished capacity of the Roman legal establishment to handle and during the late fifth and early sixth centuries a number of more simple Roman law codes were issued under the aegis of various barbarian monarchs. Thus, for example, a Burgundian Roman law made its appearance as did a more elaborate Visigothic Roman law. In the seventh and eighth centuries even more simple collections of Roman law appeared. Most of these were more or less epitomes of the Visigothic Roman law which is also called the *Breviary of Alaric.*

Through these documents it is possible to trace the history of Roman Jewry law in the Germanic kingdoms of early Medieval Europe. Thus it will be useful for students to compare and contrast these various codes with each other and also to examine the fate of Roman Jewry law under the barbarians in comparison with what it was like under the Roman Empire.

In the following pages all the laws that concern Jews which appear in the *Breviary of Alaric* have been presented. In addition, all the laws concerning Jews that appear in two of the epitomes: *The Epitome of Aegidius* and *The Monk's Epitome* have also been translated.

SELECTIONS FROM THE BREVIARY OF ALARIC—506[8]

1. In cases that concern the state as contrasted to those that concern the Jewish superstition, Jews are to live under Roman law and are to

bring suit and defend themselves according to the Roman law. In short, the Jews are under our laws. In cases of a civil nature, however, Jews are permitted, if both parties agree, to have their cases decided before Jewish judges. The judges of the provinces are to execute the decision of the Jewish courts.

All Jews who are known to be Romans are to have the cases that concern their religion handled by their judges and among themselves the Jews are to live according to Jewish Law. In cases that concern the state, Jews are to have their cases heard in the provincial court before the imperial judge according to the laws under which everyone else lives. (2.1.10).

2. We order that on the Sabbath and on all the other days when Jews carry out their religious observances they are not to be forced to do any kind of public service nor are they to be required to attend court as the result of a suit. It is clear that there are enough other days for these things to be done. (2.8.3).

3. No Jew is permitted to buy a Christian slave or to make available to ex-Christians Jewish religious ceremonies. If, however, a public investigation shows that Jews have done these things then the slave is to be taken from his Jewish owner by force and the owner is to be punished in accordance with the crime that he has committed. In addition, if any Christian slaves or slaves that were once Christian but are now Jews are discovered to be in the possession of Jewish owners these slaves are to be purchased for a fair price by Christians because Jews are not to own either Christian or ex-Christian slaves.

It is of primary importance that no Jew is to have in his possession a Christian slave. If a Jew through some means does, in fact, possess a Christian slave, then the owner is under no condition to convert the slave to Judaism. If a Jew does convert a Christian slave to Judaism then all of the Jew's slaves will be taken from him by force and he will be punished in accordance with the magnitude of his crime. Before this law was established it was the law that if a Christian slave had been converted to Judaism the owner would have to sell the slave to a Christian for the price that he had originally paid for it. This was done by the Christian buyer in order to permit the slave in question to be a Christian. (3.1.5).

4. Jewish men are not permitted to marry Christian women and Christian men are not permitted to marry Jewish women. Any person who

breaks this law is to be considered to have committed adultery. Anyone may accuse those guilty of such acts and the judges are to pay attention to rumors.

The severe punishments established by this law make it clear that Jewish men are not to marry Christian women and Christian men are not to marry Jewish women. It is further made clear that those who disobey this law and do marry contrary to it will be brought to trial and punished just as if they had committed adultery. The right to accuse people of having broken this law is not reserved to close relatives but can be exercised by anyone. (3.7.2).

5. No Jewish man is to take a Christian woman as a wife and no Christian man is to take a Jewish woman as a wife. Any person who breaks this law is to be considered to have committed adultery. The right to accuse the guilty party is granted to everyone. (9.4.4).

6. In order to cause suffering to those Christians who turn Christian altars to the use of pagan rites we take the right to make testaments from them. Those Christians who give up the Christian religion and abandon the name Christian in order to defile themselves with the diseased Jewish religion are to be punished also by losing their right to make testaments (16.2.1).

7. Jews are not permitted to harass or to attack any man who has been converted from Judaism to Christianity. Anyone who violates this law is to be punished according to the offence of which he is guilty. (16.3.1).

8. We order in accordance with the already established ancient law that any person who is converted from Christianity to Judaism and who attends their religious services is to have his property confiscated and handed over to the treasury. (16.3.2).

9. Any Jew who buys a Christian slave or a slave belonging to any other religious group and circumcises that slave must surrender the circumcised slave. The slave who has been thus treated is to be freed. (16.4.1).

10. Jews are not permitted to buy Christian slaves or to obtain them as gifts. Any Jew who breaks this law is to have the slave in question confiscated. If the slave provides the information that leads to the discovery that the law has been broken then he is to be given his freedom. A

Jew, however, is permitted to continue to keep all other Christian slaves whom he already owned even though they are of the true faith and he is the follower of a hated superstition. This condition refers only to slaves that the Jew had obtained before this law went into effect and includes those Christian slaves that he might inherit or obtain through a trust. Further, the Jew will lose the slaves if either by force or by other means he converts these slaves to Judaism. If Jewish slave owners do convert their Christian slaves to Judaism, the lawbreakers are to be executed and their property is to be confiscated. (16.4.2).

11. It has come to our attention that Jews, Samaritans, pagans and other monstrous heretics are so insane and uncivilized that they do not worship the true God. Since they are so stubborn, wicked, and arrogant our efforts to show them the truth will undoubtedly cause them to be dealt with severely and their suffering will be their own fault. (Nov. Th. III.1).

12. Since it is well known that no cure can be found for incurable diseases it is necessary to act so that the deadly evils of these sects will not spread. Therefore we establish for all time that any Jew or Samaritan who lives according to the laws of either of these sects are to be barred from obtaining any governmental offices or titles, they are not to serve in the civil administration and they are not to serve as the imperial official who watches over the city governments. We maintain that it is wrong for Jews and Samaritans who are enemies of God to serve as upholders of imperial law. Further, these people should not be protected in their evil ways by holding imperial office and they are not to have the power to judge Christians or to sentence Christians. Certainly, Jews are not to be in a position in which they can judge bishops or insult the Christian religion. (Nov. Th. III.2).

13. Also, we follow this same reasoning in ordering that no new synagogues are to be built. We do, however, permit to Jews the right to repair old synagogues that are in great need of being fixed up. (Nov. Th. III.3).

14. We add that any person who converts a free Christian or a Christian slave from Christianity to any other sect or religion is to be executed. The proselytizer is to have his property confiscated as well. (Nov. Th. III.4).

15. If any Jew or other heretical person obtains an imperial office he is to have everything taken from him that he holds or that he has gained from the position. If such a person has built a new synagogue he is to know from this law that he has done so for the benefit of the church to whom the building is to be given. If any of these people manage to sneak into a governmental position and if he has enjoyed the privileges of rank he is to know that he is to be reduced to his former position as an outsider. Any Jew who starts to build a new synagogue and is not merely engaged in repairing an old one is to be fined fifty pounds of gold and have the newly begun building confiscated. Any Jew who converts a Christian to Judaism is to be executed and he is to have his property confiscated. (Nov. Th. III.5).

16. Jews and other heretical persons are not to be permitted to avoid the public services that all Romans owe and those who try to obtain exemptions through bribery and other corrupt means are to be punished. (Nov. Th. III.6).

17. Jews and other heretical persons who are, as a result of the service that they owe to their cities, in a position to carry out the judgments of the court, are to limit their actions to enforcing sentences in cases that have been adjudicated under Jewish law. These people, in addition, are not to serve as prison guards because we do not want them to be in a position where they can make Christian prisoners suffer not only the sentence they were given but additional difficulties. (Nov. Th. III.7).

THE EPITOME OF AEGIDIUS[9]

1. Among themselves the Jews are to live according to Jewish laws. In all other matters insofar as they concern the state the Roman law is to be followed and the provincial judge is to preside.

2. No action is to be taken to disturb the Jews on their Sabbath.

3. Jews are not to have Christian slaves.

4. A Jewish man is not to have a Christian wife and a Christian man is not to have a Jewish wife. Those who do this are to be punished for adultery.

5. If a Jew takes a Christian wife or if a Christian takes a Jewish wife they are to be punished for adultery.

6. Those who give up the Christian religion and the dignity of the Christian name are to lose the right to make testaments.

7. We order in accordance with the already established ancient law that any person who is converted from Christianity to Judaism and who attends their religious services is to have his property confiscated and handed over to the treasury.

8. Any Jew who buys a Christian slave or a slave belonging to any other religious group and circumcises that slave must surrender the circumcised slave.

9. It is not permitted for any Jew or any Samaritan to perform any governmental service, nor to hold the position of imperial official who oversees the city governments, or to be a prison guard, or to build new synagogues. The above-mentioned who are enemies of our laws are not to dare to judge anyone or to sentence anyone according to our laws and if they dare to do so they are to be fined fifty pounds of gold. If they violate these laws they are to lose their property and be executed.

THE MONK'S EPITOME[10]

1. All the affairs of the Jews that they have among themselves they are to arrange according to Jewish law. In business with Christians they are to follow our laws and come before the judge of the province. If both parties in a civil suit wish to be heard under Jewish law then this is permitted and the judge of the province is to enforce the decision.

2. We order that no Jew is to be disturbed on the Sabbath either for governmental service or for any kind of business.

3. No Jew is to have a Christian slave. If a Jew does have such a slave and dares to place him under Jewish law then he is to lose the slave and suffer a punishment in accordance with the seriousness of the crime that he has committed. Before this law was enacted a Christian slave

who was converted to the filthy Jewish religion was to remain a Christian and be paid for.

4. No Jew is to take a Christian woman as a wife and no Christian man is to take a Jewish woman as a wife. If they do this they are to suffer the punishment for adultery. The right to accuse those who break this law is not reserved to close relations but may be pursued by anyone.

5. Christians who go to pagan temples or contaminate themselves with the disease of the Jewish religion are to be punished for these disgraceful acts.

6. A Jew who has been converted to Christianity is not to be attacked or harassed by the Jews. Those who violate this law are to be punished according to the magnitude of the crime. If a Christian has been converted to Judaism and attends their sacrilegious rites his goods are to be handed over to the treasury.

7. If a Jew buys a Christian slave or one from any other sect and circumcises him then the slave is to be taken from the Jew and he is to remain a free man.

PAPAL POLICY

The policies articulated by the popes concerning the Jews during the early Middle Ages had particular significance in large parts of Italy where the head of the church and his bishops exercised secular power as well as being the dominant spiritual authority. Beyond Italy, the impact of papal policy was less great. Nevertheless, the decisions made by popes had great value as precedents of authority for ecclesiastics and also for laymen who wanted to institute or enforce policies that at one time or another had enjoyed papal support.

Pope Gregory I (590-604), known as Gregory the Great, was the most influential Roman pontiff during the early Middle Ages and perhaps the most important in the history of the papacy. Fortunately, we are especially well informed about most aspects of Gregory's career and his Jewish policy is no exception. Included in this section are selections from about a third of his letters that deal with Jews. This material is important not only as an illustration of Gregory's Jewish policy, but because later popes and numerous church councils were greatly influenced by his pronouncements and the principles upon which they were based. Gregory's writings were, throughout early medieval Europe, considered to have great authority.

While studying these letters the reader should bear in mind that they are documents illustrative of real events and not abstract treatises or formal legislative enactments. They show the efforts of an important church official to deal with very real and pressing problems which, through one means or another, had come to his attention. These letters are more pragmatic than speculative, more concerned with the real than with the ideal. Students will want to examine the legal aspects of Gregory's decisions and search out the laws upon which he relied. Further, it is of importance to use these letters as a means to understand the nature of the Jewish community and its relations with secular as well as with religious authorities.

SELECTIONS FROM THE LETTERS OF POPE GREGORY I[11]

1. Joseph, a Jew who has brought certain gifts to me, told me that the Jews who live in the fortified city of Terracina have for a long time been accustomed to celebrate their religious rites in a certain place. Further, that you, dear Bishop Peter, have driven them from that place and that with your knowledge they have set up their house of worship in another place for celebrating their holidays and services. Now, however, you have expelled them from the new place. If this is true, Bishop Peter, we want you to stop harassing the Jews. They are not to have any reason to complain, and you are to permit them to gather in the place that they established with your knowledge after you expelled them from the older establishment. Indeed, it is necessary to treat those who dissent from Christianity kindly, gently, persuasively, and with information about salvation if they are to be won for Christianity. If you do not act in this reasonable manner those who might be converted by the sweetness of preaching and the vision of the horror of damnation will be driven away by threats and earthly harassment. It is better that they should come to hear the word of God from you in a friendly atmosphere. They should not be terrorized by your attacks. (1.34).

2. The Hebrews who live in Terracina have asked us for permission to continue to hold the synagogue at the place where they have held it up to now. Since this synagogue is so close to the church that the sound of the Jews' singing can be heard in the church, we have written to Bishop Peter indicating that if, in fact, the Jews' voices can be heard in the church it will be necessary for them to stop worshipping there and to move their synagogue. Thus, I want you, Bishop Bacaudius and Bishop Agnellus, to investigate the matter along with Bishop Peter and if you find that the church service is in any way bothered by the synagogue you are to provide the Jews with another place to worship inside the defenses of the city so that they can celebrate their service without any problems. Be careful that you provide them with a place that will not cause future problems. Remember, we will not permit the Jews to be harassed or bothered without reason; they are permitted to live peacefully and in security under the Roman law. They are to be permitted to follow their religion as it has been passed on to them. They are not, however, allowed to have Christian slaves. (II.6).

3. From the beginning of your tenure as the governor of Sicily, God has willed that you move in the support of His cause. His mercy has set

aside for you a reward with accompanying praise. It has been reported
to us that a certain Nasas, a very evil Jew, has with criminal rashness
built an altar dedicated to the blessed Elijah. By sacrilegious means this
Nasas has lured many Christians to worship at his altar. Indeed, he has
also, it is said, gotten possession of Christian slaves and used them for
his work and gained great profits. Yet, as we have been told in letters,
the glorious Justinus who preceded you as governor was deterred by his
greed and did not avenge this injury against God. We ask you to begin a
strict investigation of this matter and if indeed you find that what has
been reported to me is true, please hurry to punish the malefactors very
severely and inflict bodily punishment upon the wicked Jew. Do this in
such a way that you will win God's favor for yourself and show by your
example and your reward a principle to those who succeed you. Also,
set free according to the law any Christian slaves that this Nasas may
have obtained so that the Christian religion may not be defiled by being
subject to Jews. Thus, do all of these things to correct the situation
quickly and strictly so that we can give you our thanks and so that we
can indicate to any who might ask that you do your job well. (III.37).

4. It has come to our attention that male and female slaves owned by
Jews have fled to the church in the city of Caralis and that you, Bishop
Januarius, have neglected the fact that they have indicated that they
wanted to become Christians. Indeed, you have restored these slaves to
their owners or have paid them the value of the slave. Let me emphasize
that you are not to permit this evil custom to continue. Any Jewish-
owned slave who flees to the church is to be protected from retaliation.
If he was already a Christian or becomes a Christian then you must support and sustain his claim to freedom and you are not to use church
funds designated for the support of the poor to compensate the Jews.
(IV.9).

5. We have learned from many informants that Christian slaves are
owned by Jews who live in the district of Luna. This bothers us even
more than usual because you, Venatius, bishop of Luna, permit this
practice to continue with your knowledge and permission. Indeed, it is
your duty as a bishop and because of your religion as a Christian to let
no chance pass to win souls away from the Jewish superstition. You do
not have to do this by persuasion but by your authority. Thus we want
you to enforce the laws which are pious in their nature to the effect
that no Jew is permitted to have a Christian slave in his possession. Indeed, if Christian slaves are found in the possession of Jews the slaves

are to be freed by the protection of the law. Concerning Christians who work on the lands of Jews but who are not slaves, these latter people are to continue to perform the agricultural services which they owe and to do as they have always done, i.e. paying their rents and performing their services. But it is clear that no further burdens are to be imposed upon them. If these same *coloni* wish to avoid the rents and service that they owe and wish to move to another place, make it clear to them that they will lose their rights when they abandon their duties and that is rash even if it results in greater freedom. You, Bishop Venatius, must be careful not to let your flock scatter nor are you to permit wrongs to be done for lack of energy. (IV.21).

6. We have written to you previously, Bishop Fortunatus, to make it clear that if any slaves who are inspired by God wish to give up the Jewish faith and become Christians their owners are not free to sell them. Indeed, from the time that these slaves make known their wish to be Christians they have a rightful claim to be free. It has come to our attention, however, that the Jewish slaveowners at Naples have distinguished cleverly between Jewish slaves who want to become Christian as mentioned in our previous directive and pagan slaves who want to become Christian since we did not mention the latter group in our previous letter. Therefore, you are to look into this situation and see to it that any Jewish-owned slave, whether a Jew or a pagan, who indicates a desire to become a Christian is to be protected from being sold. Yet, we do not want to give the Jewish slaveowners reason to believe that we are acting against them in an unreasonable or prejudiced manner. Thus, you are to distinguish between slaves possessed by the Jews for work on their estates and in their homes and slaves transported from foreign regions for purposes of sale. If the latter indicate that they want to become Christians and flee to the church or even go as far as the front courtyard of the church, then the Jewish slave trader has three months to try to find a Christian buyer for the slave in question. If the Jew is unable to sell the slave as noted above and the slave still wants to become a Christian then the owner under no condition is to sell him but he must set him free. The three-months waiting period makes it clear that the slave trader who has not sold the slave within the stipulated time was, in fact, not interested in selling the slave but rather wanted to keep the slave as his personal possession. Remember, you must be careful to follow our instructions carefully and do not permit special pleading or influential individuals to trick you and you are not to give such people special favors. (VI.29).

7. A short time ago we wrote to Bishop Victor of Palermo because some Jews of that city complained in a petition to us that he had taken possession of certain synagogues and their guest houses in Palermo. We told Bishop Victor to stay away from the Jews until we could learn whether he was acting legally in what he did because we would not want some kind of injury to come to the Jewish community unjustly. Indeed, since Bishop Victor is a bishop, we doubt that he has done anything wrong. Yet, we have learned from the report of Salarius, who serves as a notary in our administration and who has visited Palermo, that there was no reasonable cause for Victor to have taken possession of these properties. And, in addition, he has acted too hastily and with poor advice in consecrating these holdings. Therefore, we ask you, Fantinus, as *defensor* of the city, to see that justice is done. Since it is impossible to return the buildings to the Jews because they have been consecrated, see to it that Bishop Victor pays compensation and along with the Patrician Venantius and the Abbot Urbicus ascertain the value of the synagogues and of the guest houses that were connected to them as well as the gardens adjoining them and see to it that Bishop Victor pays compensation. After your inventory of what has been taken is complete, see that all of it is in the possession of the church and that the Jews suffer no more injustice or oppression. Also see if any books or other adornments have been taken away and see that they are found and returned and let there be no cheating in this matter. Remember, the Jews are not to have permission to do anything in their synagogues which is not permitted by law and as I have written earlier nothing is to be done to them in violation of law and equity. (IX.38).

8. We have learned that you are eager, dear Bishop Fortunatus, to stop the slave trade carried on by the Jews of Naples who buy Christian slaves in Gaul. Thus, let me tell you that I am very pleased that you feel this way and also that I would like to see this activity stopped too. We have learned from the Jew named Basilius who has come to Rome with other Jews that imperial officials have sponsored this trade and that the latter have indicated which slaves the Jews should buy. Thus the Jews deal in both Christian and pagan slaves. Therefore, it has been necessary to arrange matters so that it will not seem to the imperial officials in question that we are interfering in their business. Also it would be unfair to cause the Jews an unjust expense since they claim that they are forced to obey the imperial officials. What I want you to do, Bishop Fortunatus, is the following: when the Jewish slave traders return from Gaul, they are to turn over to the imperial officials who have placed the

orders or to Christian buyers the Christian slaves whom they have transported. This is to be done within forty days of their arrival in Naples.
Thus, after forty days have passed none of these Jewish slave traders
are to have in their possession any of the Christian slaves whom they
have transported from Gaul. If, however, any of these slaves happen to
become ill so that they cannot be sold within the forty-day period they
are to remain in the possession of the Jews until they are well and then
they are to be sold. Remember, it is not appropriate for anyone who is
free from blame to suffer a loss of any kind in this business. Also, I do
not want the lack of these new procedures during the past year to result
in causing the Jews any losses. Therefore, if you have recently taken
any Christian slaves from the Jews or if the Jews possess Christian slaves
from last year's dealings, permit them to sell those they still retain and
to dispose of those which you have taken from them.

In addition, we have learned that the above-mentioned Basilius desires to give to his sons who by God's mercy have become Christians
certain slaves who are Christian. Basilius, it would seem, desires to use
this device to continue using these slaves in the same way as before except that he no longer would be their owner. This then would stop
these Christian slaves from going to the church and thereby obtaining
their freedom as is permitted for Christian slaves who are owned by
Jews. If these slaves who have been given to Basilius' Christian sons try
to gain freedom through the church you are to see to it that they are returned to their new owners. You, however, are to keep watch over the
situation so that no frauds may be perpetrated. The Christian slaves are
not to live in Basilius' house but if he wants to have their services you
must use your position to make it clear to these Christian slaves that
they are to work for the Jews because the church (and it is God's will)
must see to it that sons do as their father requests. (IX.104).

9. Those who want to convert non-Christians to Christianity and
come to their task with a pure heart should learn the method of kind-
ness rather than of harshness. Thus, it is important to make sure that
those who might be brought into the fold by sweetness and reason
are not driven away by hostility. Anyone who does not take the course
of reason in these matters but suspends the legal religious rights of such
people clearly is not acting in God's cause but in his own. The Jews of
Naples have complained to me and have asserted that certain persons
are trying to stop them from carrying out their holiday services. It is
legal for them to hold these services just as their ancestors followed

them and they must not be disturbed without reason. Indeed, if it is true that disturbers of the peace are acting in the above-mentioned manner then it is clear that they will accomplish nothing. Why should we try to set up rules for the way the Jews should observe their rites, since we cannot hope to convert them by this means? Rather, we should follow a policy of acting reasonably and kindly toward them so that they will wish to follow us rather than flee from us. If, indeed, we prove to them from their own scriptures that our teaching is correct we may, with God's help, convert them and bring them into the church. Thus, dear Bishop Paschal, do your best to interest them in Christianity with God's help and do not permit any disturbances to upset their rites. Let them be free to observe and to celebrate their holidays and feasts just as they and their ancestors have done since ancient times. (XIII.5).

GOVERNMENT, POLITICS, AND WAR

As we have seen in the legal texts presented above, Jews were forbidden to do very much of anything in the governmental arena. The repetition of legislation and the frequent laments about non-compliance with previously enacted laws makes it clear that Jews were continually involved in government and politics. From the various texts presented in this section the reader will see that Jews took part both formally and informally (legally and illegally) in virtually all aspects of political activity including the holding of governmental offices and the participation in the military organization of the various Germanic kingdoms. Thus, for example, Procopius' account of the Byzantine attack on Naples illustrates the role played by the Jews in the city garrison. The same role is illustrated in the account of the siege of Arles. From other texts, Jews are depicted acting as legates, ambassadors, legal consultants, and royal advisors.

It is clear that those who provide the evidence of such Jewish participation often cast it in a negative light. Thus, it should be remembered that the annals and chronicles of this period were more often than not written by monks and priests who in general were not kindly disposed toward the Jews. However, we must not be misled by the biases we find in the sources. It is necessary to see past the author's inclination in order to dig out the facts.

THE SIEGE OF NAPLES–536[12]

The Jews promised that the city would be well supplied and the Goths promised to defend the walls. Thus, the leaders in Naples decided that they would not surrender. Those who were besieged at Naples, however, sent a message to the Ostrogothic ruler Theodatus who was at Rome asking him for help. It had generally been Theodatus' practice, even before the present situation arose, to ask the advice of men who were known to be able to tell what was going to happen in the future.

The Hebrew told Theodatus to lock up three herds of ten pigs each in three separate sheds. The groups of pigs were then named Goths, Romans, and imperial soldiers, respectively. The pigs were to stay locked up for a few days. Theodatus did as the Hebrew advised. When the waiting period came to an end, the Hebrew and Theodatus together went into the sheds to look at the pigs. They found that eight out of the ten pigs called Goths were dead; almost all that were called the emperor's soldiers were still alive; and those called Romans lost all of their hair but about half of them survived.

As Belisarius besieged Naples from both the land and the sea he gradually became very annoyed and began to wonder if the defenders would ever surrender. The strong position of the city made it very unlikely that he would be able to capture Naples by attack. In addition, Belisarius began to worry about all the time he was spending trying to reduce Naples because he did not want to be placed in the position of having to attack the Ostrogothic monarch, Theodatus, and lay siege to Rome during the winter.

Nevertheless, Belisarius' troops managed to enter the city through the aqueduct while others attacked the northern part of the wall which surrounded Naples. On the side of the wall that faces the sea, however, the defense was in the hands of the Jews and not of the barbarians. There the soldiers were not able to use their ladders to scale the wall. The Jews, indeed, had strongly opposed the surrender of the city and had held out that it should not be given up without a fight. They had no hope if they should be captured because of their hostility and therefore they continued to fight even after they could see that the rest of the city had fallen. They held out well beyond what the attackers had expected. Finally, at daybreak, some of the attackers who were on the walls began to shoot arrows at the Hebrews from behind and at last they had to retire. By the time the Hebrews had been defeated Naples had fallen, the gates of the city were opened, and the Roman army entered.

THE SIEGE OF ARLES—508[13]

After the Frankish monarch Clovis killed the Visigothic ruler Alaric II at the battle of Vouille, the former's Frankish forces joined with Burgundian units to besiege the city of Arles. As the siege wore on, a relative of Bishop Caesarius, who was from the latter's home town and also a cleric, became very frightened that he might be captured. Because of his youth he was not steadfast in his loyalty and courage. Thus, being pushed by the devil, he acted against Caesarius who was God's servant and climbed down a rope from the walls of the city at night and surrendered the next day to the enemy who were laying the siege. When the Visigoths who ruled Arles learned what had happened they gathered a crowd along with the Jews of the city who enthusiastically shouted and charged that Bishop Caesarius had sent his kinsman who shared with him a loyalty to their home city to plot the surrender of Arles. The bishop thus was imprisoned. This pleased the devil, and the Jews of Arles happily went around claiming without any fear that they would be charged with treachery and saying all kinds of evil things about the orthodox Christians. Then one night, one of the Jews who served in the garrison for the purpose of defending the wall threw a stone from the part of the wall that he was guarding. It was made to seem that the stone was thrown at the enemy but in reality there was a note tied to it indicating the name of the man who threw the stone and the fact that he was a Jew. In the note he offered the enemy the opportunity to attack the part of the wall that the Jews guarded and told them they could set up their ladders there during the night. In return for this aid the Jew asked that after the city was taken none of the Jews of Arles should be taken as captives and that they should not be robbed of their property. In the morning, however, some of the garrison went out beyond the city wall and someone found the letter. Soon after this, its contents were made known throughout the city. The Jew was captured, tried, and punished. Thus everyone then knew the cruel wickedness of the Jews who detest both man and God. After the siege was broken and many captives had been taken, Caesarius set about ransoming Christians. The holy man of God said: "A rational man who has been saved by the blood of Christ must not lose his freedom and by being made a slave end up being converted to either Arianism or Judaism."

FURTHER JEWISH MILITARY ACTIVITY[14]

In the year 848, the Danes captured, depopulated, and burned the city of Bordeaux in Aquitaine with the treacherous help of the Jews.

In the year 851 the Moors took the city of Barcelona with the treasonous help of the Jews. After having killed almost all the Christians there and having devastated the city they withdrew without suffering any losses.

JEWS IN GOVERNMENTAL SERVICE–526[15]

Pope John returned to Rome and King Theodoric was very angry with him. In fact, the king ordered that the pope was to be considered a royal enemy. A few days later John died. After this, Symmachus, who served on Theodoric's legal staff and who also was a Jew, announced at the order of Theodoric who was now a tyrant rather than a king that on the 26th of August 526 the Arians would take over all the Catholic churches. Indeed, He who does not permit His faithful to suffer at the hands of heretics punished Theodoric just as He punished Arius who founded the religion. Thus, the king was taken ill with diarrhea and after three days of suffering gave up both his throne and his life. This was on the very same day that he had intended to take over the Catholic churches.

801-802[16]

The Muslim envoys to Charlemagne reported that the Jew Isaac whom the emperor had sent with Lantfrid and Sigimund four years before to treat with Harun-al-Rashid was on his way back to the West with a great many lavish gifts. Lantfrid and Sigimund, however, had died along the way. Charlemagne ordered his notary, Ercanbald, to go to Liguria in order to prepare a fleet of ships to transport the elephant that Harun-al-Rashid had sent. In the month of October, Isaac the Jew crossed from Africa with the elephant and arrived at Porto Venere. Since the snow blocked the Alpine passes and Isaac was not able to cross the mountains he spent the winter at Vercelli. On the twentieth of July, Isaac arrived with the elephant and with the other gifts that had been sent by Harun-al-Rashid. Isaac then turned all these presents over to Charlemagne at Aachen. The name of the elephant was Abul Abaz.

876[17]

In the name of the holy and undivided Trinity. Charles emperor and augustus by the mercy of almighty God sends greetings to all our own Barcelonians. Know that we are doing well as a gift from God and we wish that you do well also. We are sending to you, moreover, many thanks because always and in all ways you have extended yourselves faithfully for us. Accordingly, Judah the Hebrew, our loyal supporter, has come to us and has described in detail your faithfulness to us. Thus, in return for your faithfulness we are prepared to send to you a proper remuneration. Continue to extend yourselves in our behalf in all things just as you have done thus far.

877[18]

Charles, attacked by a fever, took a potion in order to heal himself. The powder was given to him by his doctor, a Jew named Sedechias, for whom the emperor had far too much friendship and much too much confidence. This powder was, in fact, a deadly poison that he had taken. The king was then carried by hand across the Alps. When he arrived at Brios he sent a message to have Richild who was not far away to come to him and she did. Eleven days after he took the poison he died in a miserable little house on the sixth of October.

AN UNPUBLISHED ORDER—855[19]

We order concerning the Jews that none of them are to remain in the kingdom of Italy later than the first day of October. They are to be informed in the appropriate manner that they are to depart by the above-mentioned date and to go wherever they might wish. No one is to interfere with their departure. Any Jew who is found in the kingdom of Italy after October first can be taken prisoner by anyone, and the Jew is to be brought to us along with whatever is in his possession.

JEWS AT THE COURT OF LOUIS THE PIOUS[20]

The Jews are especially popular at the court and it is said that the emperor values them highly because of the patriarchs. Important people at the court seek the prayers and the blessings of the Jews and they wish that they had such people to support them as those who favor the Jews. The Jews say that the Christians at the court are angry because Bishop Agobard has prohibited the use of Jewish wine. The Jews make a great deal of money from these sales. Indeed, according to the canons Christians are forbidden to eat and drink with Jews. All the time the Jews go around showing people the imperial orders that they have been given under the imperial name and seal which protect the privileges granted to them. They are permitted to build synagogues against the law. Indeed, the Jews brag about the glory of their ancestors, their wives show off clothing which they claim to be gifts from royalty and

from the ladies of the palace. Some Christians even say that the Jews
are better preachers than are the priests.

MERCHANT ACTIVITY AND LANDHOLDING

Throughout the early Middle Ages Jewish merchants played an important role in long distance commerce. Jewish communities around the Mediterranean and in the larger inland cities provided merchants with connections which traders from other groups did not have in such a well-developed state or in such a closely knit manner. After the Muslims conquered most of the eastern Mediterranean the importance of Jewish merchants in the West, especially, was greatly increased. Only the Jews could more or less easily bring goods from the Christian West to the Muslim East and return to Christian territory with valuable cargoes. It was very difficult and often impossible for Christian merchants from the West to travel and trade in Islamic lands on a regular basis and it was virtually impossible for Muslims to travel in the West.

The first text below describes the activities of the celebrated Radanite merchants who probably had their base of operations in the cities of southern Gaul near the mouth of the Rhone river. In the following texts is material gleaned from a collection of anecdotes about Charlemagne, charters to Jewish merchants from both within the empire and from outside of it, complaints about imperial support for Jewish activity that was perceived to injure Christianity, and other selected items.

The conventional view that Jews were city dwellers rather than landholders is nuanced, as we have seen, by many of the laws intended to regulate Jewish possession of slaves and Jewish relations with the agricultural workers dependent upon them. Additional information on Jewish landholding is provided by charters such as the one included here and occasionally by letters such as the one written by Pope Stephen III to Archbishop Aribert of Narbonne in about 768.

ROUTES OF THE JEWISH MERCHANTS
CALLED RADANITES[21]

These merchants speak Arabic, Persian, the languages of the Roman Empire, of the Franks, the Spanish, and the Slavs. They go from west to east and from east to west by land and by land and sea. From the west they carry eunuchs, female and male slaves, silken cloth, various kinds of furs, and swords. They ship out from Frankish territory on the Mediterranean Sea and head for Farama in the Nile delta. There they unload their ships and put their goods on camels to travel by land to Qulzum at Suez. This trip takes about five days. They then reload their goods on ships and sail on the Red Sea from Qulzum to al-Jar, the port of Medina, and then to Jidda, the port of Mecca. Then they head for Sind, India, and China. On the return trip from China they carry musk, aloes, camphor, cinnamon, and other goods from eastern lands to Qulzum and on to Farama. From there they cross the Mediterranean again. Some of the merchants sail to Constantinople in order to sell their goods to the Byzantines. Others go to the palace of the king of the Franks to sell their wares.

Sometimes these Jewish merchants take a different route when they leave the kingdom of the Franks and sail on the Mediterranean to Antioch. From Antioch. they travel to al-Jabiya. This takes three days. Then they load their goods on a boat that sails on the Euphrates to Baghdad. From Baghdad they sail down the Tigris to al-Ubullah. They leave al-Ubullah and go on to Oman. From Oman they go to Sind, India, and China.

All these routes are interconnected and links can be made overland. Merchants leaving from the Frankish kingdom or from Spain sail across the straits of Gibraltar to North Africa and then to Tangier. They cross North Africa to the capital of Egypt. From there they go toward Ramla. They stop at Damascus and then go on to Kufa, Baghdad, and Basra. Then they cross to Ahwaz, Fars, Kirman, Sind, and India. Finally, they arrive in China. Sometimes they take the route that passes on the other side of Byzantium and after crossing the country of the Slavs they arrive at Khamlij, the capital of the Khazars. From there they take ship on the Caspian Sea and go to Balkh and to Transoxiana. They continue until they reach the region where the camps of the Tughuzghur are established. From there they go on to China.

CHARLEMAGNE AND JEWISH MERCHANTS

1. One time Charles came to a port city in southern Gaul. While he was dining some Viking raiders came into sight. Some of the people in the emperor's entourage who saw the ships said that they were Jewish merchant vessels, others thought that they were Muslims from north Africa, and some said that they were British merchants. The wise Charles, however, knew from the cut of the ships and their quick movements that they were enemies and not traders.[22]

2. I have already indicated how the very wise Charles raised up those who were humble. Now I will tell you how he humbled those who were too proud. There was a certain bishop who was very vain and greedy and much too interested in all kinds of foolishness. When the very wise Charles learned about this bishop, he called one of the Jewish merchants who frequented the court. He was a man who often went to the Holy Land to trade for all kinds of valuable and strange things which he brought back from across the Mediterranean. Charlemagne then told the merchant that he was to cheat the bishop in some way to make him look very foolish. Thus, the Jew caught a house mouse and stuffed it with all kinds of spices. He offered to sell it to the bishop and told him that it was a very valuable animal that he had brought back from Judea. He added that it was not known in the West. The bishop was very happy that the Jewish merchant had given him an opportunity to buy this wonderful thing and offered him three pounds of silver for it. The Jew then remarked that three pounds of silver was not a fair price for such a remarkable thing and said "I would rather throw this little thing into the sea than sell it for such a low price. The rich bishop, who had so much money because he never gave anything to the poor or the unfortunate, said that he would give the Jew ten pounds of silver for this very rare thing. The clever Jew then made believe that he was angry and said "Let the God of Abraham not let me suffer the loss of my effort and my travel expenses in this deal." The bishop, however, became even more anxious to have the little mouse and offered to give the Jew twenty pounds of silver. The Jew then made believe that he was even more angry and wrapped up the mouse in a valuable piece of silk cloth. He then acted as though he was going to leave. The bishop was completely fooled and offered him a box full of silver for the mouse. Finally, the merchant agreed to sell it to him. Then the Jew took the money

that the bishop had given him to the emperor and told him the entire
story. Then Charlemagne called together his bishops and brought out all
of the silver that the Jew had given him. The emperor then said "One of
you bishops has paid all of this silver to a Jew for a painted house
mouse."[23]

JEWISH MERCHANT CHARTERS[24]

1. Be it known to all bishops, abbots, counts, vicars, hundred men and
our other officials that we have received by our word and that we keep
under our protection the Hebrews who came into our presence, David,
a descendant of the house of David, and Joseph with their partners, all
inhabitants of the city of Lyons. Therefore we order and we make clear
through this our charter that neither the above-mentioned officials nor
their subordinates nor their successors may dare to do anything that
might harm the aforementioned Hebrews through any kind of illegal action. In addition, you are not to institute any suits nor are you to take
possession of any of the private property that they seem to have acquired legally nor to dare to take away nor to diminish nor to generate
any suit at any time. Further, you are not to demand from the afore-
said Hebrews any toll or taxes for horses, or for housing or for damage
done to fields or for rights to dock on the river bank or carting taxes,
or taxes at the city gate or for crossing bridges or for pasturing their
animals. These Jews are to be permitted to live quietly under our defense and protection and to serve the palace faithfully. Also we concede
to them the right to make deals concerning their goods with whatever
men they might wish. Also, they are permitted to live according to their
law and to hire Christian workers to labor for them as long as they do
not require them to work on Sunday or on Christian holidays. These
Jews also have the right to buy foreign slaves and to sell them within
our empire and no faithful supporter of ours is to dare to baptize any
of their foreign slaves without the consent and the willingness of the
Jewish owner. If a Christian brings suit or has a case against these Jews
then the Christian must have three worthy Christian witnesses and also
three worthy Hebrew witnesses so that his testimony will be accepted
and so that with these witnesses he may win his case. And if these Jews
will have a suit or a case against a Christian, they must have the support
of Christian witnesses and with them they may win their case. If, indeed, anyone, Christian or Jew, wishes to hide the truth, the count of

the place in question is to hold an inquest and each one of the persons involved is to testify according to his own law. If any case arises or will arise against these Jews concerning their goods or their slaves which cannot be decided locally without serious and unjust loss let the proceedings be suspended and held over to be brought to our court where a final judgment will be made according to the law. And we wish all of you to note that as already mentioned because we have taken these above-mentioned Hebrews under our protection and defense that as long as they remain our faithful supporters anyone who advises that they be killed or anyone who kills them will have to pay ten pounds of gold to our palace treasury. Further, let no one dare to subject these often mentioned Hebrews to whipping unless this has been the judgment according to their own law. The capitularies that have been issued on these matters by us and for them are to be observed and those who have violated them or provoked their violation in which this same provision is defined are to be coerced by whipping for their guilt. (no.31).

2. Be it known to all bishops, abbots, counts, vicars, hundred men and our other officials that we have received by our word and we keep under our protection a certain Hebrew named Abraham from the city of Saragossa who has come into our presence and commended himself into our hands. Therefore, we order that this charter of protection of ours be given to Abraham. With this document we make clear and we order that neither any of you [the officials mentioned above] nor any of your subordinates nor any of your successors are to dare to do anything that might harm the above-mentioned Jew by any kind of illegal action. In addition, you are not to institute any suits nor are you to take possession of any of his personal goods nor to interfere with his business in any way at any time. Further, you are not to collect any tolls, nor taxes for horses, nor for housing nor for damage done to fields nor for rights to dock on the river bank nor carting taxes, nor taxes at the city gate nor for crossing bridges nor for pasturing their animals. He is to be permitted to live in peace under our protection and our defense and to serve the palace faithfully without anyone doing anything illegal to the contrary. The Jew is permitted to live according to his laws and to hire Christian workers to do his work any time except on Sunday and on Christian holidays. If a Christian has to bring a suit against him, the Christian must bring to court three worthy Christian witnesses and also three worthy Jewish witnesses so that his testimony will be supported and with these witnesses the Christian can win his case. If Abraham has

a suit or a case against a Christian, he must produce worthy Christian
witnesses in support of his position and with them he may win his case.
If anyone, either a Christian or a Jew, wishes to hide the truth, then the
count of the city is to institute an investigation to find the truth and do
justice and each party involved is to answer according to his own laws.
The Jew, Abraham, is to be permitted to buy foreign slaves but he is
not to sell them except within the limits of our empire. If, indeed, any
suit will have come up or arisen against him or against any of his men
which looks bad for him according to the laws and that cannot be settled locally without unjust and serious loss, action is to be suspended
and the case is to be held until brought to us so that final judgment can
be made at the palace according to the law. So that these privileges will
be believed to be authentic by everyone and so that they may be preserved accurately, we order this document to be signed according to
custom and sealed with our seal. (no.52).

3. To all bishops, abbots, counts, administrators on royal estates, vicars,
hundred men, officials in charge of frontier posts, our agents in the
field and no less to all our faithful supporters both present and future
—be it known that we have taken under our protection and that we
hold under our protection the Hebrews, Rabi Domatus and his nephew
Samuel. Therefore, by this document we make clear and we order that
neither you [the officials to whom the document is addressed] nor
your subordinates nor your successors are to dare to do anything that is
illegal to harass the above-mentioned Hebrews or to start suits against
them, or in any way or at any time to take or to diminish their private
property which they were seen to possess legally. In addition, do not
dare to demand from these already mentioned Hebrews any toll or tax
for horses, nor for housing nor for damage done to fields, nor for rights
to dock on the river bank nor carting taxes nor taxes at the city gate
nor for crossing bridges nor for pasturing their animals nor for catching
fresh fish. Similarly, we give them the right to make deals concerning
their own property so that they may sell to whomever they wish. Also,
they are to be permitted to live according to their own law and to hire
Christian workmen to do their work except on Christian holidays and
on Sunday. They have the right to buy foreign slaves and to sell them
within our empire. If a Christian has a case or a suit against these Hebrews then he will have to produce three worthy Christian witnesses
and also three Hebrew witnesses to support his testimony and with
these witnesses he can win his case. If these Hebrews have a case or a

suit against a Christian, they must produce some Christian witnesses to support their testimony and with these witnesses they can win their case. These same Jews have told our highness about certain men who, contrary to the Christian religion, persuade slaves that are owned by Hebrews to condemn their lords under the protection of the Christian religion and to be baptized. In addition, they are persuading them to be baptized so that they may be freed from the service of their lords. The holy canons do not support these actions. Indeed, they judge that perpetrators of such things are to be sentenced to severe anathema. Therefore, we wish that none of you [the persons to whom the document is addressed] dare to do anything like this to the above-mentioned Hebrews or permit your subordinates to do anything like this and you had best be certain that they follow this order because anyone who does anything like the above and we are told about it will not be able to escape without facing great danger to himself and the loss of his property. And we also wish you to note this as already mentioned because we have taken the above-mentioned Hebrews under our protection and defense for as long as they remain our faithful supporters , and anyone who advises that they be killed or who kills them knows that they must pay ten pounds of gold to our imperial treasury. Further, we wish that the above-mentioned Jews in no way are to be subjected to any judicial examination, i.e. neither by fire nor by hot water nor even by whipping except as it may be permitted to them as they live under and follow their own law. (no.30).

THE COMPLAINTS OF BISHOP AGOBARD[25]

Indeed, I have suffered because of those at court who support the Jews. They are angry because I preached that Christians should not sell Christian slaves to Jews and that Jews should not be permitted to sell Christian slaves in Spain. They are also angered because I have preached that Jews should not be permitted to hire Christian domestic workers and because I have tried to stop the Jews from having these women who are Christians work on Sunday and celebrate the Jewish Sabbath. I also preached against Christians who dine with Jews and eat meat during Lent because of this. Further, I preached that Christians should not eat meat that was slaughtered and skinned by the Jews. Christians should not buy and drink the wine that the Jews make and sell. In fact, Christians should have nothing to do with Jews.

Yet, imperial agents have changed the market day from Saturday to Sunday so that the Jews will be able to keep their Sabbath.

I have learned from a certain man who fled from Cordoba in Spain that he was stolen by a Jew from the region of Lyons twenty-four years ago when he was a little boy and sold as a slave to the Muslims. He said that he escaped along with another man who was stolen by a different Jew at Arles only six years ago. We have learned from other sources that other Christians have suffered the same fate of being stolen and bought and sold by Jewish slave dealers. We have also learned that many Christians are sold by other Christians to Jews and that the latter do things to them that are so ugly that I cannot write about them.

SOME LEGISLATION CONCERNING JEWISH MERCHANTS[26]

1. Merchants, that is Jews and the other merchants, whether they come from this country or from other countries, are to pay a fair toll on slaves as on other goods just as it has always been under the kings in earlier times. (no.253, ch.9).

2. Concerning circumcised merchants and other merchants, that is the Jews who pay a tax of a tenth and the Christian merchants who pay a tax of an eleventh. . . (no.281, ch.31).

JEWISH LANDHOLDERS

1. It belongs to us who have received the key to heaven through the apostolic succession to present the remedy of the divine faith to the diseased multitude. This is why we were greatly tormented and, indeed, almost shocked to death when we learned from you, Bishop Aribert, in your letter, that the Jewish people who are always rebels against God and who attack our ceremonies possess within the boundaries and territories of Christian-dominated places hereditary tenure to lands in the towns and in the area around the towns just as do Christians through charters granted by the kings of the Franks. Some Christians cultivate the vine and the fields owned by the Jews. Christian men and Christian women live under the same roof with these liars and are contaminated day and night by their words of blasphemy. These unfortunate men and women must humble themselves like dogs. Indeed, have not the promises made to the ancestors of the Hebrews by their chosen legislator Moses, and his successor Joshua been fulfilled in every way by our

Lord? Indeed, the promises given to these unbelievers and to their criminal ancestors ought to be taken back in order to avenge the death of the crucified Savior. The leader of the church counseled the orthodox people when he wrote: "it is not possible to bring together the light and the shade without drawing into a pact Christ and the devil."[27]

2. In the name of the Lord God and of our Savior Jesus Christ, Louis by divinely propitiated clemency emperor and augustus. Although apostolic teaching reminds us especially to do good for our brethren in the faith, it does not prohibit us from doing kindnesses also to all the rest. But it exhorts, rather, that we pursue humbly the course of divine mercy. Therefore we order that the above-mentioned Hebrews, Gaudiocus and his sons Jacob and Vivacius, and their descendants may possess and hold through this our charter the aforementioned estates with all that pertains to them and all that is a part of them, that is, with the houses and all the rest of the buildings, and the cultivated and uncultivated land, and the vines, and the fields, and meadows, and the water and the running water, and the mills and all rights of exit and entering and reentering without any opposition or any rights being withheld. They also are to hold by proprietary right with the power to dispose or to do as they wish in that they have the power to sell or to give or to commute and in all matters pertaining to the land and whatever is attached to it. Let no one dare to generate any kind of false suit or start any kind of disturbance concerning any of the above-mentioned matters but the aforementioned Hebrews are to hold the said things securely and peacefully. So that this conformation of our charter will remain firm and inviolate, and unchallenged by custom we sign it and order our seal to be affixed to it.

Given on the VIII Kalends of March in the twenty-sixth year of the empire of the most pious lord augustus Louis by the grace of Christ. Done at the royal palace at Frankfort happily in the name of God. Amen.[28]

THE LOCAL POLITICAL SCENE

The political role played by Jews in the royal governments of the early middle ages was as we have seen buttressed by their economic importance. Most Jews, however, were not part of the king's entourage or important merchants who transported goods across half the globe. During this period the vast majority of Jews in the West lived in the cities and their rural environs. These cities were in many ways miniature city states in which local politics and local factions were often of greater importance than the royal or imperial governments. We have seen from the legislative evidence that the efforts of the central power, such as it was, to have its will be done was frequently thwarted at the local level.

On the local scene the Jews as a group either acting in concert with other non-Jewish elements of the population or on their own can clearly be discerned in the surviving sources. This is well illustrated, for example, by the texts presented here concerning the factional strife at Clermont. Gregory also provides us with an illuminating example of Christian-Jewish cooperation, intrigue, and murder in the handling of city finances. From the cities of Italy we also obtain a picture of factional violence at the local level and a clear indication of how Jews at the royal court influenced the situation on the local scene. This was also true in the Carolingian empire.

With some understanding of the relation between local and central political power the reader will find himself better able to develop an appreciation of the complexity of the historical scene in general but more importantly new and more varied meanings will be gleaned from the legal sources presented earlier. Also the reader must keep in mind that much of this material comes from contemporary accounts of events that were recorded by clerics who generally did not appreciate the Jews. It should become clear that documentary evidence, while not free of bias, provides very different kinds of data than do the narrative sources.

THE STRUGGLE AT CLERMONT [29]

Bishop Cautinus of Clermont had buried the priest Anastasius alive to get his lands. The latter escaped and told his story to the king. While Anastasius spoke with the king, Cautinus entered the court. When Anastasius accused him the bishop left defeated and beaten. This Cautinus was neither pious nor reflective but illiterate in both secular and religious matters. He was, however, on very close terms with the Jews and he was very much under their influence. He did not work to convert them, which is the task of a good bishop, but relied upon them to sell him valuable objects. He was one of those people who is easily flattered and the Jews gave him the attention that he wanted. Then they sold him these valuable things at much greater prices than they were worth.

When Bishop Cautinus died at Clermont there were many who wanted to succeed him. The priest Eufrasius, who was the son of the dead Evodius, a man of the senatorial class, obtained a large collection of valuable objects from the Jews and he sent these to the king. Beregisil, Eufrasius' relative, brought the gifts in the hope that he could gain by bribery what he did not justly deserve. The clergy at Clermont, however, chose the archdeacon Avitus and he went to the king also. Count Firminus of Clermont opposed Avitus and sent some friends to get the king to postpone his choice and offered 1000 pieces of gold. The king, however, refused all the offers. Thus it happened that the people of Clermont gathered in one place and chose Avitus. The archdeacon was elected by the clergy and the people, as I said before, to the bishop's seat.

Because it is God's way always to give glory to His bishops by His grace, I am going to tell you what happened to the Jews of Clermont in 576. The holy Bishop Avitus often urged the Jews to look beyond the Law of Moses and to learn the true spiritual meaning of the scriptures. He wanted them to discover with pure hearts the holy teaching of Christ, the Son of the living God — that which is promised by the prophets. Although the Jews remained stubborn, the bishop prayed and finally one of them asked to be baptized during the holy week of Easter. He wanted to be reborn in God by the sacrament of baptism. Thus, dressed in a white robe he went in a line with all the other catechumens. As the procession was going through the city gate a Jew, at the urging of the devil, poured rancid oil on the head of the convert. The bishop, however, stopped the mob from stoning this Jew. On the very holy day that the Lord ascended in glory after having saved mankind, the bishop was leading his flock from the cathedral to the basilica, the whole crowd that was following him attacked the Jewish synagogue and leveled it to the ground. A few days later Avitus sent a message to the Jews saying: "I will not force you to believe in the Son of God. All I do is preach His virtue to you. I am like a shepherd who is sent by the Lord to look after His sheep. Indeed, the true shepherd said of you that He had sheep who were not in His fold that He wanted brought in so that there would be one flock and one shepherd. Therefore either you Jews will believe as I believe, and become part of one flock with me as your shepherd or you will leave Clermont." For three days the Jews could not decide what to do and then they decided, I think due to the actions of Bishop Avitus, and sent this answer to him: "We believe that Jesus is the Son of the living God who was promised to us by the prophets." Avitus was very happy when he received the news and after celebrating the evening service he went to the baptistry outside of the city walls. There a whole crowd of Jews lay down in front of him and asked to be baptized. His eyes were filled with tears of joy at the sight and he washed each Jew and anointed each with holy oil and brought them into the church. He baptized more than five hundred Jews. The rest of the Jews of Clermont who refused to receive baptism went to the city of Marseilles.

CONFLICT AT RAVENNA [30]

While King Theodoric was at Verona a conflict broke out between the Jews and the Christians of the city of Ravenna. This happened because the Jews of the city who had no wish at all to be baptized frequently mocked the holy water that was offered to them and threw it into the water of the river. This made the people of Ravenna very angry and ignoring the king and the consul Eutharicus and Bishop Peter, they attacked the synagogues of the city and set them on fire. At about this same time a similar uprising took place at Rome.

After this happened some of the Jews went to Verona to see the king. There, the king's chamberlain, Triwane, who was a heretic, also favored the Jews. He convinced the king to take action against the Christians. Thus King Theodoric ordered that the Romans of Ravenna who were orthodox Christians were to provide the funds to rebuild the synagogues of Ravenna that had been burned down. Those Christians who did not have any money were to be whipped through the streets of the city and an official was to go in front of them announcing what they had done. This, in effect, was the order that was given to the consul Eutharicus, to Cilliga, and to Bishop Peter. They carried it out.

TROUBLE AT ROME[31]

It is necessary that civilized conduct which is the basis of Roman life be followed in the city of Rome. It is fundamentally uncharacteristic for Romans to act like the foolish mobs of other cities and burn their own city. We have been informed by Count Arigern, nevertheless, that the people of Rome became very angry at the punishments that had been meted out to some Christian slaves who had murdered their Jewish owners. The mob then burned the synagogue to the ground and thus foolishly vented its anger on innocent buildings because it was furious with the men who use them.

Thus it is important that you immediately punish very severely those few leaders who incited the mob to carry out this violence. Also you should look into the complaints that have been made against the Jews and if you discover that they are well-founded, then punish them according to the law.

PROBLEMS AT MILAN[32]

It is necessary if civilization is to be preserved that the workings of justice not be denied even to people who are well-known to have taken the wrong direction concerning religion. You have complained that your rights concerning the synagogue are not being enforced. Thus we make it clear that you are to have the full protection of royal power and we order that no church official is to encroach on the privileges granted to your synagogue nor are ecclesiastics to concern themselves with the affairs of your community. The two communities of orthodox Christians and Jews are to be kept separated because their faiths are so different. But remember you are not to do anything of an uncivilized nature against the rights held by the church.

FINANCE, INTRIGUE, AND MURDER[33]

In 584, a Jew called Armentarius along with another Jew and along with two Christians came to the city of Tours to receive payment of a debt owed to them by two former royal officials. These were Injuriosus, who had been a vicar, and Eunomius, who had been a count. This debt was in the nature of a loan to these men for which they had given as security their share of the royal taxes which they were empowered to collect. When Armentarius presented his demand for payment, Injuriosus and Eunomius promised to pay back the principal that had been advanced to them as well as the interest that was owed. They said that they would go to their house and that he should follow them. Then they said: "If you come to our house we will pay all that we owe to you and give you additional gifts that you deserve for your service." Armentarius went to their house and he was welcomed by Injuriosus, who invited the Jew to dine with him. After the meal was over, they went to another room in the house. Now it is rumored that the two Jews and their two Christian partners were murdered by Injuriosus' armed retainers and that the bodies of the murdered men were thrown into a well near the house. The kinsmen of the murdered men heard what had happened and came to Tours. Here they got some information from certain unnamed persons and found the well. They dragged up the bodies from the well. Injuriosus, however, claimed throughout all of this that he knew nothing about the matter. He was brought to court, however. Since he denied his guilt, and since there was no direct evidence against Injuriosus which could convict him, the court declared that he could clear himself by taking an oath. The kinsmen of the murdered men, however, refused to be satisfied with the decision of the court and brought their search for justice to the king's court. Indeed, neither the money that had been owed to Armentarius nor the papers recording the debt could be found. Many people claim that the tribune Medard also was mixed up in the affair, since it is known that he too borrowed money from the dead Jew. In any event, Injuriosus went to the king's court and as is the custom he waited for the plaintiffs to bring their charges for three full days until sunset. The plaintiffs, however, did not appear at King Childebert's court and since Injuriosus was not charged he returned home.

CONFLICT AT LYONS

1. A short time ago I visited the imperial court to present my complaints concerning the Jews in my diocese. You, Adalard, Wala, and Helisachar heard me out and reported to the emperor while I waited outside in the anteroom. He refused to hear me and only sent me away.

I am writing to you now so that you may advise me what to do about the pagan slaves who are owned by the Jews. Our emperor does not worry about baptizing by force the pagans whom he conquers why should we not also baptize the slaves within the empire? These slaves whom the Jews own we are willing to pay for according to the law and thus they will not lose any money. Yet, the Jews refuse to sell us their slaves and say that they do not have to do so because they are favored by the judges at the imperial palace. I would like to have your support in this and through you an order from the emperor. Indeed, this whole business would not have taken place if the master of the Jews had followed your orders in the first place. If this master of the Jews had acted as he should have and had shown the proper respect for my position as it is my aim to act toward him in the proper manner, then no injury would have been caused through the interrogation that took place at the court. If the master of the Jews had acted reasonably then there would be no conflict concerning the suits brought by the Jews.

If I do not baptize the Jews and the Jewish-owned slaves who ask to be baptized, then I fear that I will be damned by God. If, however, I do perform these baptisms then I am in danger because I will have broken imperial law and by this I will cause serious damage to be done to the church.[34]

2. Your imperial agents Garric and Frederic came here at the request of Evrard the master of the Jews and acted very harshly toward the Christians and very friendly toward the Jews. In fact, they have persecuted the church of Lyons and caused cries of lamentation to be voiced by faithful Christians.

This began when the Jews gave me a document under your name and also gave one to the viscount which ordered him to support them against me. In fact, these documents were made known to all as imperial orders by the viscount who read them in public. Although these documents appeared under the imperial seal, I refused to believe that you could have ordered them.

The insolence of the Jews has become absolutely unbearable. They enjoy the injuries caused by your agents. When Evrard came on the scene he made it clear that you were hostile to us because of the Jews. Now your agents are here with more imperial commands that I still do not think have been sent by you.

Good Christians are on the run or in hiding. The rest who daily see and hear these things are shaken in their faith. Worse yet, the Jews' case has won out, and they dare to go around preaching irreverently to Christians and blaspheming the Lord God and the Holy Savior Jesus

Christ in front of Christians. Their perversity is strengthened by the documents brought to Lyons by your agents.[35]

3. I am writing to you, Hilduin and Wala, because you are both very close advisors to the emperor. This letter concerns a woman who was converted from Judaism to Christianity and who because of this has been very seriously harassed. The Jews have in their possession a document which they contend was granted to them by the emperor and which indicates that no one is to baptize a Jewish-owned slave without the permission of its owner. I cannot believe that such an order could have been issued by our so very pious Christian emperor because it is fundamentally contrary to the canons. Indeed, by this legislation the emperor helps the unfaithful Jews in their treachery. These Jews never freely permit anyone to become a Christian but both publicly and privately blaspheme those who are true believers. Thus, I am trapped here between two great dangers. If I obey the emperor's order then I certainly will offend God. If, however, I do not obey the command then I will offend the emperor. Indeed, the master of the infidel Jews has threatened me and made it clear that imperial agents from the palace will be sent at his request to see to it that I do as the order commands.[36]

JEWS IN EARLY MEDIEVAL SOCIETY

The texts presented in the previous sections have tended to unite around particular themes such as government or trade. Yet, in examining these sources carefully the reader can see that the materials were not concerned exclusively with the particular topics indicated by the section titles. In this section the texts may be considered to consist only of the very general theme of Jews in early medieval society. In a sense many of these texts bring together aspects of previous chapters. If any one theme comes through here it may perhaps be a slight emphasis on relations between Jews and Christians.

FROM THE LETTERS OF SIDONIUS APOLLINARIS[37]

1. In this letter, Bishop Eleutherius, I recommend a Jew to you. I do not do this because I support their erroneous beliefs but because it is not right to consider Jews to be completely lost as long as they still live. Indeed, anyone who is alive is a potential object of conversion and thus is capable of being saved. I think it is better that the bearer of this letter tell you himself in a personal interview about the troubles that have beset him. It is consistent with good letter writing not to clutter them up with wasted words. It is best to be concise and to remind you that the Jews, when it comes to non-religious matters, and particularly in legal questions, often have very good cases. Thus, even though you are a bishop it is perfectly reasonable that you defend this man's rights even though you may attack his treacherous religion. (VI.11).

2. Gozolas, who is of the Jewish people, and also one of your men, my dear friend Felix, brings this letter to you. Indeed, he is a person whom I would very much like, if I did not so detest his religion. I have written this letter to you with a great deal of anxiety because of the armed bands of fighting men which rove around the outside of our city. This is because we here are a kind of frontier outpost between the Burgundians

and the Visigoths. We are suspected of disloyalty by the former, and
the latter make us suffer because we are seen by them to be loyal to the
former. (III.4).

3. Again I am sending my greetings to you dear Felix through the same
man as before. Your man Gozolas (may God see fit some day to make
him our man by converting him to the true faith) thus is for a second
time the bearer of my letter. Please answer this letter so that you will
not seem to insult both me and the bearer of the letter and give people
the idea that you think we are unworthy either to receive your letters
or to carry them. Let me hasten to add that I am not asking you, as I
did before, to discuss the present state of affairs since I do not want to
put you in the position of having to commit yourself on the situation
and then have you find that you had been wrong. (IV.5).

4. Because, dear Bishop Nunechius, I am very enthused by all of the
good things that I have heard about you, I am taking this opportunity
to recommend to you the bearer of this letter named Promotus, whom
you used to know but who now, through your prayers, has become one
of us. Although he is by birth of the Jewish people he can now be considered an Israelite because of his faith rather than because of his blood.
He sought citizenship in the City of God through the Holy Spirit and
rejected the killing stagnation of the Hebrew Law. He weighed the reward of salvation against his future as a Jew which meant eternal suffering and thus he converted from circumcision to Christ. He has decided
that the New Jerusalem rather than the old is to be his fatherland. Now
let the spiritual Sarah embrace him as a truer son of Abraham because
he ceased to be a follower of the slave Hagar when he abandoned his
dedication to the Jews' Law and accepted the freedom given by God's
grace. He will tell you the remaining details and indicate why he is coming to your diocese. Let me mention that he is very dear to me because
he has been saved. (VIII.13).

THE JEWS OF GENOA[38]

1. In response to your request, know that the Jews of Genoa are permitted to put a new roof over the old walls of their synagogue. They
are not to expand the size of the synagogue, however, nor are they to
add any decorations. If they violate these limitations they are in danger
of incurring the king's displeasure. (II.27).

2. The basis of civilization is the observance of law. This is what separates men from animals and makes life in groups possible. Therefore we are very happy to grant your request that we renew all the privileges that were guaranteed to you by past laws which protected Jewish customs. (IV.33).

THE JEWS AND THE KING AT ORLEANS[39]

On his way to Paris, King Guntram detoured and stopped at Orleans. The day that he entered Orleans was the feast of Saint Martin, the fourth of July, and huge crowds of people came out to meet the king with flags and banners. They sung various songs praising him. In one place you could hear Syrians speaking their language, in another place the Latin speakers could be heard and even the Jews were in the crowd. All these languages mixed together in a cacophony of sound as each group hailed the monarch with shouts of "long live the king," and "let Guntram's rule over the kingdom last for uncounted years." The Jews who were seen to take part in this welcome shouted repeatedly, "Let all the peoples adore King Guntram and bow to you and be your subject." The only result of the Jews' praise was that after mass the king said, "Nothing good will happen to the Jews. They are always evil and faithless and in their hearts they are very sly. They hailed me and flattered and praised me and shouted that everyone should bow to me as their lord because they want me to rebuild at public expense their synagogue which the Christians destroyed a while ago. May the Lord not let this happen. Indeed, I will never rebuild it." Our glorious ruler who is so praiseworthy in his wisdom guessed at what the clever Jews were planning and when these faithless people came to him afterwards and asked that he rebuild their synagogue they did not gain anything from their show of support.

A JEWISH FEUD[40]

In the year 582, King Chilperic ordered the baptism of some Jews. He acted as godfather to many of them and received them from the baptismal font. Some of these converts were washed only physically but not spiritually. In fact, they lied to God and returned to their faithless practices. Thus while they gave the appearance of observing the Lord's day they still observed the Sabbath. There was no argument, however, by which the Jew Priscus could be led to accept the truth.

The king was so angry that he ordered him to be thrown into prison and intended to force Priscus to listen and to believe even if he would not do so freely. First, Priscus tried to dissuade the king by giving him valuable presents and obtained a delay so that he could attend the marriage of his son who was to marry a Jewish woman from Marseilles. Priscus, in fact, falsely promised the king that he would accept baptism after the wedding was over. During the period of delay, however, Priscus got into a fight with Phatyr, one of the Jews who had been converted. He was a godson of the king. On the Sabbath, when Priscus was on his way to the synagogue, wearing his prayer shawl and unarmed, he and his followers were attacked by Phatyr and his men, who cut down their unarmed opponents. Phatyr and his followers then took sanctuary with his armed band in the Church of Saint Julian, which was near the place where the attack had been carried out. While they stayed at Saint Julian, Phatyr's men learned that the king intended to spare their leader but that they were to be taken from the church and killed. By this time Phatyr had already left the church. So one of his men took his sword and killed his companions. Then he left the church with his sword unsheathed and was attacked by a mob of townsmen who killed him in a very painful manner. Phatyr obtained royal permission to return to Guntram's kingdom where he lived. A few days later, however, Priscus' kinsmen caught up with him and killed him.

A JEWISH DOCTOR [41]

An archdeacon from Bourges named Lunast lost his sight. He visited many doctors but he could not get any better. Finally, he visited the church of Saint Martin at Tours where he stayed for two or three months. There he prayed and fasted regularly in order to get his sight back. When the feast of Saint Martin arrived, Lunast's eyes were cleared and he could see once again. When he returned to Bourges he went to see a Jewish doctor who bled him for the purpose of strengthening his sight. As soon as the blood had been taken, the archdeacon once again lost his sight. I believe that he lost his sight because of his sin. As John has it, "Behold, you have been made whole. Sin no more or worse things might happen to you." This man Lunast would have remained healthy if he had not gone to see the Jew after he had benefited from God's miraculous power. It is about men like Lunast that the apostle warns when he says "Do not be yoked together unequally with unbelievers because the righteous and the unrighteous do not belong together."

SUNDAY vs. SATURDAY[42]

While Saint Owen was riding through the region of Anjou he learned of a man who ground grain into flour. The latter, while working on Sunday, had an accident and part of the dowel upon which the millstone turned broke off and became imbedded in his hand, causing his thumb nearly to be severed to the accompaniment of a great deal of blood. A great crowd was attracted, and it was seen that no one could withdraw the dowel from the man's hand. Then the poor man went to the holy man and confessed that he had broken the Lord's day and violated the Lord's commandment. When the holy man saw this, he was moved by pity for the poor man, made the sign of the cross over the damaged hand, and asked the Lord to make the man healthy once again. Then the holy man warned and advised him that for the health of his soul he was not to do any kind of physical labor on the Lord's day. He then remarked that the Jews observe the Sabbath because of the Lord's commandment and since this was the case it was necessary even more so that Christians who have been saved by His blood should observe the day of the Lord.

JEWISH REACTION TO A MIRACLE[43]

A great crowd of people came together in a great hurry at the little palace chapel where the relics of the Saints Marcellinus and Peter were kept to see the miracle by which a girl who had lost the power to control her arms and legs recovered with God's help so she once again had full use of her limbs. Among the many people who witnessed this miracle were a number of Jews, one of whom was named David. After he had seen the miracle, David went to the little cell where I was and called to me through the little window. He told me about the miracle and gave thanks to God who, acting through the medium of His martyrs, was willing to perform such wonders for the benefit of mankind.

A BISHOP COMPLAINS[44]

I have been traveling throughout my diocese making it clear that according to God's law and according to the canons, Christians are not to have anything to do with those who do not have the true faith. These include not only the pagans who live along with the Christians but also the Jews who live in the city of Lyons and throughout our diocese. Indeed, some Christians are known to observe the Jewish Sabbath and to work on Sunday. The Jews have many Christian slaves working in their homes and these slaves are corrupted so that they follow Jewish religious practices.

BODO[45]

Bodo, an Alaman noble who was a deacon at the imperial palace, abandoned Christianity and converted to Judaism. He was advised and influenced by treacherous Jews at the palace and became a professed Jew. He was circumcised, let his hair and beard grow, and changed his name to Eleazar. He put on the habit of a fighting man, married the daughter of a Jew, and saw to it that his nephew became a Jew also. Because of greed he went to the city of Saragossa in Spain in the middle of August. The emperor Louis, however, had great difficulty believing that Bodo had done these things.

After a few years, this Bodo, who had renounced the truth of Christianity and abandoned himself to the infidelity of the Jews, believed so fully in this evil that he worked to incite the Saracens against the Christians in Spain. It was Bodo's aim to force all the Christians in Spain either to convert to the follies and stupid beliefs of the Jews or of the Muslims. Then there came to King Charles and to all the bishops of his kingdom the pitiful request of the Christians of this kingdom that he force this apostate to stop tormenting these Christians who live in his territory and stop making them die.

DISPUTATION AND POLEMIC

From numerous sources it is clear that confrontations between Christian and Jewish preachers, proselytizers, and scriptural commentators were not an uncommon phenomenon. It would be misleading, however, to imagine that there were daily street corner debates. The surviving evidence would seem to suggest that city dwellers would not be shocked to learn that a disputation had recently occurred or that one was planned. Sometimes, as the text presented here indicates, a disputation could be spontaneous. More often than not, information about a disputation survives only from the Christian source, although the Jewish side is occasionally represented. It should be noted, however, that the party which preserved the record of the disputation usually represented its own side in the best light—a natural enough human practice.

In a literary sense, the record of a disputation, real or imagined, served primarily a polemical purpose. Within this framework, polemic may be considered to have had a didactic aspect as well. Among the many kinds of materials which were intended to combat the spiritual enemy and teach about his weaknesses, while defending and teaching of one's own strengths, were sermons. Jewish polemic may not have been less well developed than Christian polemic, but we know a great deal less about it. In general, the Jews were in a weaker position politically than their Christian opponents. This made it difficult for them to popularize their criticism without facing serious dangers during most of the middle ages and even in the modern era.

From the materials presented here the reader should be able to gain a good idea of how fundamentally divided were Jews and Christians in matters of religion. Each group vigorously attacked the basic tenets of the other's beliefs. Jews systematically denied the divinity of Jesus and often portrayed him as (literally) a bastard. Christians attacked the Jewish attachment to the Law and claimed that it rendered Judaism spiritually dead.

A DISPUTE BEFORE THE KING[46]

King Chilperic was at the royal villa of Nogent and was preparing to leave for Paris. I, Bishop Gregory, had gone to visit him for the purpose of saying goodbye to him when a Jew called Priscus entered. The king treated Priscus in a familiar manner because the Jew used to help him obtain precious objects. The king then took Priscus gently by the hair and said to me: "Come over here, bishop, and place your hand upon this one." The Jew resisted and then the king said: "You have a hardened soul, you are part of a people that will always be unbelievers because you do not understand what the prophets have, in fact, promised. Indeed, the mysteries of the church are to be found in its own sacrifices." The Jew answered: "God does not need a son, He did not have a son, and no one helps Him to rule His kingdom. Remember, the Lord said unto Moses: 'Look. I am the Lord and there is no other except Me. I will kill and I will make life. I will hurt and I will heal.'" The king then answered him and said: "In a spiritual manner, God had born an eternal Son. He is neither younger than God nor does He have less power. God Himself said of His Son: 'I have begotten You from the womb before the morning star.' This Son, who was born before the beginning of time, God sent to save mankind. As the prophet said: 'He sent His Word and saved them.' Your contention that He did not have a Son is contradicted by your prophet Isaiah who indicates that the Lord said: 'Is it fitting that I who have others beget not beget Myself?' Now God said this about those people who through faith are reborn in Him." The Jew answered: "How can it be that God becomes man, or that God can be born from a woman, or that God can suffer lashing, or that God can be sentenced to death?" The king then became silent and I entered the discussion. I said: "God, that is the Son of God, was made as a man because we needed Him, not because He had to. Indeed, if He had not come in mortal form He could not have saved mankind from the bondage of sin or from enslavement by the devil. Now just as David killed Goliath, I will show you from your own scriptures and not from the Gospels or from the apostles in which you do not believe and thus I will skewer you with your own sword. Your own prophet foretells that God will be made man when he said: 'He is both God and man and who has known Him?' Also the prophet Baruch said: 'This is our God, and no other is to be compared with Him because He has found the way to all knowledge and He has shown the way to His servant Jacob and to His beloved Israel. Afterward, He showed Himself on earth and spoke with men.' From the words of the prophet Isaiah: 'Look, a virgin will conceive and have a son, and He is to be called Emmanuel. To us this name means God.' It is clear that He was born by a virgin. As it is found in Psalms: 'They pierced My hands and My feet; they divided up My clothes among themselves. They fed Me bitter gall and gave Me vinegar to drink.' This makes it clear that He was beaten and pierced with nails and that He suffered many injuries. When David said that the Lord reigned from a tree, he was saying that He would save His worldly kingdom from the devil by suffering on the wooden cross. He received a new kingdom comprised of those whom He saved from the devil, but that is not to say that He did not reign before this with the father." The Jew answered: "What need was there for God to suffer all these things?" I then said: "I have already told you that God created man as innocent but that he [man] was trapped by the evil cleverness of the serpent and was led to sin against the Lord's command. Thus man was thrown out of the Garden of Eden and condemned to labor on earth. But by the death of Christ, God's only Son, man was brought back to God the Father." To this the Jew replied: "Indeed, could not God have sent prophets or apostles to direct man back to the road to salvation and thus avoid having Himself suffer in human form?" I then answered: "Man was corrupt from the start. The Flood could not scare him, nor the destruction of Sodom, nor the plagues that were visited on Egypt, nor the parting of the Red Sea nor the dividing of the waters of the Jordan. Man has always failed to accept the law of God and equally failed to believe the prophets. Indeed, they have not only disregarded the warning of the prophets but murdered those who advocated repentance. If God did not come to earth Himself to save man he could not have been saved. We have been reborn by His birth. We have been washed clean by His baptism. We have been healed by His wounds. We have been raised up by His resurrection. We have been glorified by His ascension. As your prophet Isaiah said: 'By His hurt we are healed. He will carry the burden of our sins and pray for the sinners. He was brought like a sheep to the slaughter, but as a lamb before her shearers is dumb, so too He, when He suffered His judgment, was lifted from us. His name is the Lord of Hosts.'"

Despite these and many other arguments that I made, the miserable Jew was not, so far as I could tell, moved at all. Nevertheless, he kept quiet. The king also saw that my arguments had no impact upon the Jew and thus asked for my blessing and departed for Paris.

SELECTIONS FROM THE SERMONS OF CAESARIUS OF ARLES

1. He took on human form, was born to a virgin, set in a manger, and wrapped in swaddling clothes. He was condemned by the Jews and persecuted by them. He was captured by them, beaten, spat upon, given a crown of thorns, served vinegar and gall to drink in order to take away our sins and to free us from hell. (10).

2. Through the work of the devil, who worked through Judas, the secular monarchs and the leaders of the Jews together with Pilate condemned Christ to death. (11).

3. Christians must attend church on Sunday. Indeed, the unhappy Jews celebrate the Sabbath with such great piety that they do no servile work on that day. In light of this, Christians must certainly do nothing except worship God on Sunday so as to save their souls. (13).

4. If we do not believe that we can imitate the Lord, at least we can try to imitate the blessed James who was also stoned by the Jews. James, nevertheless, bled upon his knees and prayed for his persecutors. (37).

5. Once again I ask you and beg you to come to church every Sunday. Also, I beg you to come to church on the important holy days. Indeed, my fellow Christians, it is shameful and evil for Christians to neglect Sunday while the Jews observe their [Saturday] Sabbath so devoutly. These unhappy Jews do not dare to do any kind of servile work on the Sabbath. Must not we Christians who were redeemed not by gold and silver but by the blood of Christ be very careful to observe the Lord's day and think very seriously about the salvation of our souls? (73).

6. My fellow Christians, I have told you frequently that the lessons which are read in church should not be understood primarily in their literal sense, but that it is necessary to see the spirit of salvation that is presaged by the story. Remember the Apostle who said: "The letter kills, but the spirit gives life." The unhappy Jews and the even more unhappy heretics understand and accept only the letter. Therefore they remain spiritually dead because they do not accept the life-giving spirit of scripture. (83).

7. When Abraham offered his son Isaac as a sacrifice he was a sort of symbol of God the Father. Isaac therefore presaged our Lord and

Savior Jesus Christ. The arrival of Abraham and Isaac at the place where the sacrifice was to take place on the third day is to be understood as representing the Trinity. The two servants whom Abraham ordered to stay with the ass symbolize the Jews because they could not go up to the place where the sacrifice would take place. They could not do this because they refused to believe in Christ. The ass symbolizes the synagogue. One reads the words "sit with the ass" because the Jews refuse to believe in Christ and therefore could not stand because they refused to accept the support of the staff of the cross. Indeed, the blessed priest, Saint Jerome, wrote that he had learned from old Jews and from the elders among the Jews in the Holy Land that our Lord Jesus Christ was crucified in the very place where Abraham ordered Isaac to be sacrificed. (84).

8. Those who pay close attention to scripture will learn how the usual situation is reversed and in the case of the Christians and the Jews, the elder is made to serve the younger. The Jews are shown to serve the Christians because the former have spread divine law all over the world by making their books available to all peoples. Thus, the Jews were scattered all about so that this learning would be available to all and so that Christians could point to the Jewish books and show that the prophets had all foretold the coming of Christ. If the pagans say that the Christian scriptures were not written by the Holy Ghost but by men we can show them the Jews' books, the writing of our enemies, to show that our books are supported. I certainly cannot be charged with having written the Jews' books. Therefore, I can tell the pagans to read the Jews' books and when they find that their books and our books agree, I can tell them to abandon their unbelief and to begin believing. It is in this way that the elder clearly serves the younger. (86).

9. When Isaac sent his son to a far-off land to find a wife he may be seen as a kind of God-the-Father type. This is because God the Father rejected the synagogue and sent His one begotten son to establish a church among the gentiles. (87).

10. My fellow Christians, you should know that God never rained down any manna on the Jewish sabbath because the Jews did not deserve that any manna should come to them upon their sabbath. On Sunday, however, manna always is rained down upon us and, indeed, manna first came to us on the Lord's day. Because manna comes only to Christians

we must lament and deplore the unhappy Jews because they are not worthy of receiving manna as their father once did. Indeed, they never eat any manna. The Jews cannot eat manna because they are unable to eat anything that is small or fine. They can digest nothing that is spiritual in nature. They see in scripture only the adornment and the bulk and miss the spiritual meaning of God's word. (102).

11. In all the books of scripture it is plain to see that the synagogue came first and then the church. It is also clear that the church would have far greater glory than the synagogue. Indeed, it is well known that this point is illustrated not once, or twice, or three times in the writing of the Jews, but very frequently. It appears so often that even a man who is not very wise or not very educated can see it clearly and without confusion. Indeed, my fellow Christians, it is the case that the synagogue is damaged by the light of Christ which brightens the church. This light which illuminates the heart and soul of Christians blinds the unhappy Jews. The light of Christ makes the Christians joyful and the Jews suffer. To the faithful Christian it brings salvation; to the unfaithful Jew it brings punishment. Indeed, the Jews were noticed by God before the gentiles, but later the gentiles came to God's attention and received greater blessings. Because the Jews were ultimately to be rejected by God and the Christians were to be chosen for God's grace, the first tablets bearing the law were broken but the later ones remained whole. Even at the beginning it was the younger son Abel who was God's chosen one and the elder son Cain was condemned. By remembering these truths you will be able to explain to Jews and to pagans the mystery of Christianity. We hope, however, that we will live such a just life that Jews and pagans will, as we read in the Gospel, "see our good works and give glory to our Father in heaven." (104).

12. My fellow Christians, if we faithfully and studiously do as the Lord commands, then those things that have been promised to the Jews as material rewards will come to us as spiritual rewards. All the blessings of God that they receive on earth we have received through baptism. The Jews think that when the Lord says "I will give you rain at the proper time," it is to be understood in a material sense. Thus, we must ask the Jews that if rain is a reward to those who obey His commandments why is it that the very same rain falls upon those who do not keep the commandments? (105).

13. When we read that Christ was "in the middle" it should not be understood to mean that He was between the Old and the New Testaments and therefore part of neither one. Rather it is to be understood to mean that He is in the midst of both in a spiritual sense. This clearly is not following the letter which destroys heretics and Jews both, but according to the spirit which gives life to Christian understanding. The two men who brought the grapes presage the synagogue and the church. Since the Jew came first and the Christian followed, the Christian kept salvation in front of him while the Jew let it fall behind him. In the prophet we read about the Jews: "Let their sight grow weak so they cannot see and let their backs always be weak." Thus the two men continue on carrying their holy burden; the Christian always keeps his eyes on it but the Jew always leaves it behind him. The Christian enjoys the sacred gift but the Jew is weighed down by it. Indeed, as Christ is the Savior of the believer He is a burden to the Jew. (107).

14. Eliseus' disciple Giezi can be understood to have presaged either Judas or the Jews. Giezi prefigures the Jews because he got leprosy at the same time that the gentiles got rid of it. Also, during the Lord's Passion, the unhappy Jews cried out: "His blood is on us and on our children." Thus they certainly deserve to be stricken by the leprosy of sin. When the teaching of the apostles went to the gentiles only the leprosy of sin stayed upon the miserable Jews. (129).

15. The rich man, by which we are to understand the Jews, says that he has five brothers. This means the Jews who live under the law of Moses, which has five books [i.e., the Pentateuch]. Abraham, however, said that they will not believe even if someone rises from the dead and this means that they reject Christ. My fellow Christians, as we think about these truths, let us have mercy for the poor so that we may deserve to be crowned by the Lord on the day of judgment. (165).

16. The Jews have kept the Law locked up in their minds, and its spiritual meaning was hidden away in a secret place. John was imprisoned and the Law was hidden in the hearts of the faithless as though it too was imprisoned. John's execution indicates that the letter of the law, which was but a shadow, was to die with the coming of grace and a spiritual understanding. (218).

A TRACT BY ELEAZAR, A CHRISTIAN WHO BECAME A JEW, CONCERNING THE MESSIAH AND THE CHOSEN PEOPLE — THE JEWS[48]

A letter from someone recently came into my hands that is full of blasphemies against the true and living God. I would have preferred not to have answered this letter but my tutors and teachers urged me to do it. I myself was at one time a member of the same faith as the author of this letter. But I left that condemned, base, false, cursed, horrible, despicable and vile religion. I chose the true and glorious religion and converted from the religion of idolatry to the religion of one God. In order to merit eternal reward, I have vowed to remain constant as a follower of the Law of the Lord. I believe that it is foolish to answer the barking of all these mad dogs, but I think that perhaps a little spark might kindle a little fire of faith in you; I think it is a good thing that you know that you err.

The Christians do not worship one God, but three gods. The Jews, by contrast, follow the word of the Scripture which says: "Listen, Israel, The Lord is our God, the Lord is One," and also where it says: "You do not have any God before Me," and again from the prophet: "I am first and I am last and there is no God but me."

Indeed, you Christians have converted yourselves to the worship of a man and you are the ones who are intended by the prophet who says: "Cursed is the person who believes in a man." He was a man, not God, and those who do not deny the cross and his death go to hell. This is the fate of he who follows the Book of Deuteronomy where it is written: "Cursed by God is he who hangs from the wood."

You say that your Jesus was born of a virgin. Then tell me how flesh can be born by flesh and not be violated? Would not this child who passes through the virginal walls have kissed the lips of the genitalia and defiled them?

Is it not true that you Christians make your houses for the worship of Jesus bigger than the houses made by the gentiles to their gods? Indeed, did not one of them lament on the subject: "Oh, I am so unhappy because I see that the chapels and the noble temple are already in ruins?" But you Christians are much worse than these pagans, because they did not know the Law, and God did not demand answers from them and He did not command them.

We continue to wait for the Messiah because He has not yet come. He was born, however, on the very day of the destruction of Jerusalem.

The Messiah is now held captive by chains of fire and iron. But He will come at the time that has been announced by the prophet Daniel. You Christians object to this according to Genesis where it is written: "The sceptre will not be taken from Judah and from the prince of his blood until the Messiah comes." Because you say that when Jerusalem was destroyed, the children of Israel no longer held the sceptre. But I would ask you then which sceptre did the children of Israel have and which prince led them during the seventy years that they were in captivity under Nebuchadnezzar. I would answer you myself and tell you that it is a matter of "shebet" and of "meh'akek," which is to say "tribe" and "teacher" in Latin. Often you Christians subvert the words of the scriptures with other interpretations. Thus, where Isaiah says: "Behold, a young woman will become pregnant and give birth to a son," you say: "Behold, a virgin. . . ." and many other things like that.

Your Jerome, whose translation of the scripture you use, has the Psalms all set out word for word; however, in the rest of the book of scriptures he made a false translation. Only among the Jews can one find the entire accurate text of scripture and only from this text can a completely correct interpretation be made. Among you Christians there are as many different meanings as there are translations. We Jews have only a single text of the scriptures and only one religion. I myself have seen in the palace of the kings of the Franks fourteen Catholic men with as many faiths among themselves.

You Christians always call upon the witness of the Law and of the prophets to make your arguments. I would ask you then if you have such faith in the Law why do you not observe it? But, what does the Law matter to you Christians who are animated only by the love of money and who are captives of your passion for sex? Indeed, how rare it is to find a chaste layman. Your clerics are glorified to have for themselves the amorous embraces of a great variety of women in the church itself.

Because you lead a dissolute life, you say that the Law has no force. But the Law has not been annulled, the Law that was written by the finger of the Lord, the Law about which the Lord said in the Book of Deuteronomy: "Put these words that I say to you in your heart and in your soul." Again, in the same book it is written: "Moses has given the Law to us who are the heirs of the house of Jacob." Also in the same book it is written: "Take good care not to forget the things that your eyes have seen and that they do not leave your heart all the days of your life." Listen you Christians to what has been written: "All the

days of your life" and take good care lest seeing you do not see and
hearing you do not understand.

THE LIFE OF JESUS[49]

A worthless man named Joseph Pandera who nevertheless was very
handsome spent his time robbing people and debauching. He lived in
the town of Bethlehem. Nearby a widow and her daughter Miriam lived.
The latter is mentioned in the Talmud and was a hairdresser. Miriam
was betrothed to a very pious man named Jonathan.

Joseph [Pandera] used to pass by Miriam's house and after he saw
her he wanted very much to go to bed with her. Therefore he hung
around Miriam's house a great deal and when her mother asked him
why, he said that he was madly in love with the girl. The mother then
indicated that she would not stand in his way and told him to see if
Miriam was interested. Joseph continued to hang around the house and
one Sabbath evening he found Miriam sitting outside. After a while
they went into one of the bedrooms. She thought that Joseph was Jonathan and told him that he should not touch her because she was men-
struating. He was not bothered by this and during the night he ardently
pursued his desires and made love to the girl.

Three months later Jonathan learned that Miriam was pregnant and
asked his teacher Simon ben Shetach what he should do. The latter
wanted to know if Jonathan suspected anyone and learned that Joseph
was the probable seducer. Then Simon ben Shetach told Jonathan to
find a witness and hide near Miriam's house because Joseph would
probably be back. Jonathan, however, chose rather to run away.

When Miriam gave birth to her son she named him after her mother's
brother and called him Joshua. Later on she sent him to a teacher and
the child learned well because he was not unintelligent. One day, however, the boy came into the presence of the elders in Jerusalem and did
not follow the custom of taking off his hat and bowing down. In fact,
he uncovered his head and bowed down only to the leader of the group.
There was a vigorous reaction to this, and people said that he was a
bastard and the son of an adulteress. Then Simon ben Shetach said that
he was the illegitimate son of Miriam and Joseph. This was made known
and he was declared to be unfit to be a member of the congregation.
After this he was called Jesus, which indicates that all memory of him
should disappear.

After this, Jesus left Jerusalem and settled in the [province of] Galilee. When the information that Jesus was a bastard reached his new home, he secretly went to Jerusalem and entered the Temple. There he learned the secret name of God. Then, so that he would not be frightened into forgetting the secret name of God, as were all others who had left the Temple after learning it, he wrote it on a piece of parchment. Then he cut a hole in his arm [i.e., sleeve?] and hid the parchment there.

However, Jesus could not have gotten into the Temple if he had not had some sort of magic to help him. Therefore it is clear that he was helped by the devil. Nevertheless, when Jesus left the Temple, the roar of the Lions frightened him into forgetting the secret name of God just as they had frightened all the others. After Jesus left Jerusalem, however, he opened up the hole in his arm and took out the parchment and memorized the secret name of God.

With his new power, Jesus went back to his home town and said that those who called him a bastard were themselves bastards. "I am born of a virgin and my mother conceived me in the top of her head. I am the son of God and Isaiah spoke of me when he said that a virgin shall conceive." The crowd that gathered told him that if he wanted to show them that he was God he had better back up his claims with a miracle. Jesus then ordered a dead man to be brought to him. The people dug up a skeleton; Jesus assembled the bones, covered them with flesh, and stood the man up alive. A short time later he cured a leper. The people fell to the ground and worshipped him as the son of God.

When this news reached Jerusalem, the mob of worthless louts rejoiced and the true believers wept. The elders planned to lure Jesus to Jerusalem so that he could be tried and punished. Jesus agreed to come to Jerusalem if the elders who had once called him a bastard would come to worship him. This was agreed, and Jesus set out for the city. On the way he obtained a donkey and on the outskirts of Jerusalem the people rushed out to meet him. He told them that it was of him that Zachariah spoke when he said: "Your true king will come to you on an ass bringing your salvation." The mob wept for joy and tore their clothes.

While this was happening, the pious elders went to Queen Helen and asked her for permission to deal with Jesus. They promised her that they would deal with him cleverly so that there would not be any trouble. The queen, however, wanted to save Jesus from the elders because she was related to him and so she had him brought to her court.

Then she said that she wanted Jesus to perform some miracles. He cured a leper before the court and also raised a man from the dead. Then the queen said that the charges of sorcery against Jesus were false and she let him go free.

The elders then decided that it was necessary for someone to learn the secret name of God so that he could combat Jesus. Judas volunteered to do it. Then Judas learned the secret name in the same way that Jesus had and hid it in the same way so that he could learn it after he left the Temple. Then Judas went out into the streets of Jerusalem and began saying to one and all: "Where is that bastard who says that he is the son of God? I am only a plain human being and I can do the same things that he can do."

When this matter became well known the queen called them to the royal court and the following disputation took place.

Judas:	"Jesus cannot do anything that is miraculous. Let him go up to the stars and I will bring him down."
Jesus:	"Is it not true that you have all been a bunch of stiff-necked people from the beginning?"
Judas:	"You bastard son of an adulteress, can you deny that you do evil things?"
The Bastard:	"Did not my great ancestor David say about me 'The Lord said you are my son. I have begotten you.' I will go to my father and you, Judas, will not."

After saying this, Jesus said the secret name of God and in a puff of wind was lifted up. Then Judas also said the magic name and he too was lifted up by the wind. Both Jesus and Judas floated between earth and heaven. Then Judas said the magic name again and tried to hurl the wretched Jesus to the ground. Jesus did the same and the two men wrestled in the air. Finally, their sweating made them dirty and they fell to earth.

Jesus was sentenced to death. He then said: "David, my ancestor, prophesied concerning me 'For your sake we are killed.'" When Jesus' followers and the mob learned that he was in danger they rioted and he escaped. Jesus went to the Jordan, washed off the sweat, and once again was able to perform miracles by saying the magic name. He made stones float on the water and he caught a lot of fish to feed the mob.

When the elders learned of Jesus' power and popularity they wondered who would dare to try to take away the magic name from the bastard. They promised a great reward to any hero who would do this. Judas again volunteered for the mission and went in disguise to join the mob of rabble who followed Jesus.

In the middle of the night God put the bastard into a deep sleep. Then Judas went into his tent and cut the parchment with the magic words on it out of Jesus' arm. Jesus then sent the mob to Jerusalem to fight so that he could at the same time hide among them, sneak into the Temple, and learn the magic words again. Jesus' followers then swore an oath to be loyal to him. They did not know, however, that Judas was in the crowd in a disguise.

When the mob arrived in Jerusalem, Judas reported to the elders what had happened. He told them that he knew that Jesus planned to visit the Temple, that he had 2,000 men with him, and that Jesus had taken an oath from the mob. Judas then said that on the next day he would bow down in front of Jesus and that would be the signal for the elders to attack. Simon ben Shetach and the rest were very pleased and promised to follow Judas' plan. The next day the armed citizens captured Jesus. When his followers saw that they could not recapture him, they withdrew, weeping. Then the Jews pushed their attack vigorously. Thus, after capturing the bastard they killed many of his men. The rest fled into the mountains.

Jesus was brought into the city, where he was tied up and beaten. His miracles did not help him and a crown of thorns was placed on his head. The bastard asked for water but he was given vinegar instead. Then he cried out that his ancestor David prophesied that he would ask for meat and be given gall, that he would get vinegar for his thirst. Jesus wept: "My God, my God, why have you forsaken me?"

Jesus was brought before the court and they sentenced him to be stoned and then to be hanged. Thus on Friday afternoon, before Passover began, they took Jesus out and stoned him to death. The Jews then tried to hang the body on a tree but all the branches broke under his weight. His followers claimed that it was a miracle but it was only that Jesus earlier had cast a spell over the trees because he knew that according to Jewish law he would be hanged. Judas then brought out a big cabbage stalk which was not made of wood and they hung him on it. Later they buried him where he had been stoned according to the law.

One of Jesus' followers went to the grave and wept. When Judas saw this, he moved the body and buried it in his garden. The next day when Judas found Jesus' followers weeping at the original grave he asked them what they were crying about. He then told them to look in the grave. They looked and found that the body was gone. Then the crowd said that he had gone up to heaven.

The queen learned about the execution, called in the Jewish elders, and wanted to know what they had done with the man who had been accused of being a sorcerer and a seducer. They told her that he had been buried according to the law. Then she ordered that the body be brought to court. When the elders could not find the body and told the queen that it had been stolen, she said that Jesus was the son of God and that he had gone up to heaven just as it had been prophesied. The wise men begged her not to say such things and argued that he was a sorcerer who was the bastard son of an adulteress. Then the queen told them that if they brought his body to her she would agree that they were right, but if they failed to do so they would all be killed. She gave them three days to find the body.

The elders prayed and ordered that a fast be carried on for three days. The body, however, was not found. Many people fled from Jerusalem. When one of the elders was walking in a field he came upon Judas, who was eating when he should have been fasting. The elder was surprised to learn that Judas did not know what was happening. The latter then asked if the Jews would be safe if the body was found. Then the elder and Judas went to the garden where the body had been reburied. It was dug up, tied to the tail of a horse, and dragged into the court. There it was thrown down in front of the queen. She was told that this was the man she said went to heaven, and the queen was quite embarrassed. When the body was being dragged through the streets some of the hair was pulled out and that is why today monks shave the hair from the middle of their heads.

ABBREVIATIONS

AHR: *The American Historical Review.*

JQR: *The Jewish Quarterly Review.*

MGH: *Monumenta Germania Historica.*

  AA: *Auctores Antiquissimi.*

  Epist: *Epistolae.*

  LL: *Leges.*

  SRG: *Scriptores Rerum Germanicarum.*

  SRM: *Scriptores Rerum Merovingicarum.*

  SS: *Scriptores.*

PAAJR: *Proceedings of the American Academy for Jewish Research.*

PL: *Patrologiae Cursus Completus: Series Latina,* ed. J. Migne, Paris, 1844-1864, 221 vols.

WHJP: *The World History of the Jewish People: second series, Medieval Period–Dark Ages,* vol. 11, ed. Cecil Roth, et al. London, 1966.

NOTES

1. The texts presented below were selected from *Theodosiani libri xvi cum constitutionibus Sirmondianis et leges novellae ad Theodosianum pertinentes,* ed. Th. Mommsen and P. Meyer, Berlin, 1905, 2 vols. The numbers in parentheses at the end of each selection refer to book, chapter, and enactment, respectively.

2. The texts from the Council of Toledo are to be found in *Concilios Visigóticos e hispano-romanos,* ed. José Vives, Tomás Marín Martínez and Gonzalo Martínez Díaz, Barcelona-Madrid, 1963. The letter c. and the number following it after each selection refer to the canon number.

3. The selections from the Merovingian councils are to be found in *MGH, Concilia, Aevi Merovingici,* I, ed. F. Maasen. Hannover, 1893.

4. The selections from the Visigothic laws were drawn from *Leges Visigothorum, MGH, LL,* I, ed. K. Zeumer, Hannover, 1902.

5. *Leges Burgundionum, MGH, LL,* II, ed. I. De Salis, Hannover, 1892.

6. *Capitularia Regum Francorum, MGH,* I, ed. A. Boretius and V. Krause, Hannover, 1883.

7. These selections have been reconstructed from a large variety of sources. Many of these are to be found in the section on Jewish merchant activity.

8. *Lex Roman Visigothorum,*ed. G. Haenel, Leipzig, 1849.

9. *Ibid.,* pp. 34, 44, 74, 82, 179, 248, 250, 258.

10. *Ibid.,* pp. 35, 45, 75, 83, 178, 249, 251.

11. Gregory, *Epist., MGH, Epist.,* I, II, ed. p. Ewald and L. M. Hart-
mann, Berlin, 1891-1899.

12. Procopius, *Opera Omnia,* 2nd ed., ed. J. Haury and G. Wirth, Leipzig, 1958, vol. II, pp. 45-54, *passim.*

13. *Vita Caesarii episcopi Arelatensis libri duo, MGH, SRM,* III, ed. B.
Krusch, Hannover, 1896.

14. *Annales de Saint Bertin,* ed. Felix Grat, *et al.*, Paris, 1964.

15. *Anonymus Valesianus, MGH, AA,* IX, ed. Th. Mommsen, Berlin,
1892.

16. *Annales Regni Francorum et Annales Q.D. Einhardi,* ed. F. Kurze,
Hannover, 1895; materials selected from the years 801-802.

17. *Recueil des actes de Charles II le Chauve,* ed. G. Tessier, Paris,
1952, II, no. 417.

18. *Annales de Saint Bertin.*

19. *Capitularia Regum Francorum, MGH,* II, ed. A. Boretius and V.
Krause, Hannover, 1897, no. 219, ch. 2.

20. Agobard, *Epist., MGH, Epist.,* V, ed. E. Dümmler, Berlin, 1899,
no. 7.

21. Adapted and translated from Ibn Kurradadhbah, *Le Livre des
routes et des royaumes,* ed. and trans. by M. J. de Goeje, Leiden, 1889,
pp. 114 ff.

22. Notker, *Gesta Karoli Magni Imperatoris, MGH, SSRG,* n.s., ed. H.
Haefele, Berlin, 1959, II. 14.

23. *Ibid.,* I.16.

24. *MGH, Formulae Merovingici et Karolini aevi,* ed. K. Zeumer, Hannover, 1886.

25. Agobard, *Epist.*, no. 7.

26. *Cap. Reg. Fr.*, II.

27. Stephen, *Epist.*, *PL*, 129, col. 857.

28. *Recueil des Historiens des Gaules et de la France*, ed. M. Bouquet, rev. ed., Paris, 1870, vol. VI, no. CCXXXII.

29. *Gregorii episcopi Turonensis, Libri Historiarum, MGH, SRM*, I, pt. i, ed. B. Krusch and W. Levison, Hannover, 1951. This material has been selected from Bk. IV, chs. 12, 35 and Bk. V, ch. 11.

30. *Anon. Vales.*, XIV, 81-82.

31. Cassiodorus, *Varia, MGH, AA*, XII, ed. Th. Mommsen, Berlin, 1894, IV. 43.

32. *Ibid.*, V. 37.

33. Gregory of Tours, *Hist.*, Bk. VII, ch. 23.

34. Agobard, *Epist.*, no. 3.

35. *Ibid.*, no. 7.

36. *Ibid.*, no. 6.

37. *Sidonii Apollinaris, Epistulae et Carmina, MGH, AA*, VIII, ed. C. Luetjohann, Berlin, 1887.

38. Cassiodorus, *Varia.*

39. Gregory of Tours., *Hist.*, Bk. VIII, ch. 1.

40. *Ibid.*, Bk. VI, ch. 17.

41. *Ibid.*, Bk. V, ch. 6.

42. *Vita Audoini, MGH, SRM*, V, ed. W. Levison, Hannover, 1910, ch. 9.

43. *Translatio et Miracula Sanctorum Marcellini et Petri auctore Einhardo, MGH, SS,* XV. 1, ed. G. Waitz, Hannover, 1887, Bk. IV, ch. 3.

44. Agobard, *Epist.,* no. 9.

45. *Annales de Saint Bertin.* The selection is from the years 839 & 847.

46. Gregory of Tours, *Hist.,* Bk. VI, ch. 5.

47. *Sancti Caesarii Arelatensis Sermones,* ed. G. Morin, Maredsous, 1937-1942, 2 vols.

48. This text is a selection from *Eleazari ex Christiano Iudei Tractatus de Messia Exspectando et de Electione Iudeorum,* which was reconstructed by Bernhard Blumenkranz, "Un pamphlet juif médio-latin de polémique antichrétienne," *Revue d'histoire de philosophie religieuses,* XXIV, 1954, 401-403.

49. *Toldoth Jeshu,* which is known popularly as *The Jewish Life of Jesus* was first published in English translation by Richard Carlile in *The Gospel According to the Jews called Toldoth Jesu,* London, 1823, and then in a German translation by R. Clemens, *Die Geheimgehaltenen oder sogennannten apokryphischen Evangelien,* Stuttgart, 1850. These works in turn owe something to the first Latin translation of the *Toldoth Jesu* published in Johann Wagenseil, *Tela Ignea Satanae,* Altdorf, 1681. The basic study of the many *Toldoth* texts with critical editions and translations in German remains Samuel Krauss, *Das Leben Jesu nach jüdischen Quellen,* Berlin, 1902. The selection presented here has been adapted and translated from the above works. It has been severely edited with much paraphrasing. The aim throughout has been to provide the reader with the flavor of the controversy.

SELECT BIBLIOGRAPHY

Altmann, Berthold, "Studies in Medieval Jewish History," *PAAJR*, X, 1940, 5-98.

Bachrach, Bernard S., "A Reassessment of Visigothic Jewish Policy," *AHR*, 78, 1973, 11-34.

Baer, Yitzhak, F., *Galut*, trans. R. Warshaw, New York, 1947.

Baron, Salo, *A Social and Religious History of the Jews*, 2nd ed., vols. III and IV, New York, 1957.

Blumenkranz, Bernhard, "Anti-Jewish Polemics and Legislation in the Middle Ages: Literary Fiction or Reality?" *Jewish Social Studies*, XV, 1964, 125-; 40.

—————, "The Roman Church and the Jews," *WHJP*, 11, 69-99.

Braude, W. G., *Jewish Proselyting*, Providence, R.I., 1940.

Cabaniss, Allen, "Bodo-Eleazar: A Famous Jewish Convert," *JQR*, XLIII, 1953.

Katz, Solomon, "Pope Gregory the Great and the Jews," *JQR*, n.s., 24, 1933, 113-136.

—————, *The Jews in the Visigothic and Frankish Kingdoms of Spain and Gaul*, Cambridge, Mass., 1937.

Kestenberg-Gladstein, R., "The Early Jewish Settlement in Central and Eastern Europe: Bohemia," *WHJP*, 11, 309-312.

Kisch, Guido, *Jews in Medieval Germany*, Chicago, 1948.

Langmuir, Gavin, "Majority History and Post-Biblical Jews," *AHR*, XXVII, 1966, 343-364.

—————, "Anti-Judaism as the Necessary Preparation for Anti-Semitism," *Viator*, 2, 383-389.

Parkes, James, *The Conflict of the Church and the Synagogue*, London, 1934.

—————, *The Jew in the Medieval Community*, London, 1938.

Rabinowitz, J. J., *Jewish Law: Its Influences on the Development of Legal Institutions*, New York, 1955.

Rabinowitz, L., *Jewish Merchant Adventurers: A Study of the Radanites*, London, 1948.

Roth, Cecil, "Jewish History for Our Own Needs," *The Menorah Journal,* XIV, 1928, 419-434.

—————, "European Jewry in the Dark Ages: a Revised Picture," *Hebrew Union College Annual,* XXIII, 1950, 151-169.

—————, "Economic Life and Population Movements," *WHJP,* 11, 13-48.

—————, "Italy," *ibid.,* 100-121.

Schirmann, F., "The Beginning of Hebrew Poetry in Italy and Northern Europe," *ibid.,* 249-266.

Schwarzfuchs, S., "France and Germany under the Carolingians," *ibid.,* 122-142.

Sharf, Andrew, *Byzantine Jewry from Justinian to the Fourth Crusade,* London, 1971.

Starr, J., *Jews in the Byzantine Empire, 641-1204,* Athens, 1939.

Ziegler, A., *Church and State in Visigothic Spain,* Wash., 1930.

Zimmels, H. J., "Scholars and Scholarship in Byzantium and Italy," *WHJP,* 11, 274-281.

Zuckerman, A., "The Political Uses of Theology: The Conflict of Bishop Agobard and the Jews of Lyons," *Medieval Studies,* III, 1970, 23-51.